Court Martial and Military Matters

Court Martial and Military Matters

Brig. Nilendra Kumar
Dy. Judge Advocate General
HQ Central Command, Lucknow

Foreword by
General VP Malik
PVSM, AVSM, ADC
Chief of the Army Staff
Chairman, Chiefs of Staff Committee

Manas Publications
New Delhi-110 002 (India)

Manas Publications
(Publishers, Distributors, Importers & Exporters)
4858, Prahlad Street,
24, Ansari Road, Darya Ganj,
New Delhi-110 002 (INDIA)
Ph.: (O) 23260783, 23265523, (R) 27131660,
Fax: 011 - 23272766
E-mail: manaspublications@vsnl.com
Web site: www.manaspublications.com

2004
Rs. 495/-

ISBN 81-7049-106-1

Typeset at
Manas Publications

Printed in India at
R.K. Offsets, Delhi
and Published by Mrs Suman Lata for
Manas Publications, 4858, Prahlad Street,
24, Ansari Road, Darya Ganj,
New Delhi - 110 002 (INDIA)

Dedicated to my father Sri Abinash Chandra Chaturvedi, Chief Engineer (Retd.), Minor Irrigation Department, UP and former Chairman, Institution of Engineers (India), UP Centre, and my mother Smt. Pramilla Chaturvedi for their inspiration and encouragement.

सेनाध्यक्ष

CHIEF OF THE ARMY STAFF

FOREWORD

1. The Indian Army today faces the challenges of the entire spectrum of conflict, with Low Intensity Conflict at one pole and Nuclear Warfare at the other. These challenges can be faced only by a well trained, motivated and disciplined army. It is in the context of motivation and discipline that justice has its relevance. Justice has to be administered to the men in uniform in a fair, humane and effective manner.

2. Also, there has been sea change in the social and cultural milieu prevailing in the nation. The Army, being a microcosm of the nation, has not been insulated from these changes. Military Law, therefore, has to take stock of the latest developments in the spheres of human rights, disputes redressal, gender justice, professional conduct as well as effective in-house remedies.

3. I am happy to note that Brigadier Nilendra Kumar, Joint Judge Advocate General has displayed keen interest in undertaking a detailed analysis of various legal issues of practical relevance to the Armed Forces. The book is apparently the work of a dedicated professional, deeply committed to fair play, equity and our own higher value system. The author has been able to discuss the complexities of modern legal thought as pertaining to the military canvas. His book can be easily assimilated.

4. This book no doubt would be of immense interest as a reference work, not only for students of Military Law, but for commanders at all levels, research scholars, academicians and others interested in the study of law. I wish success to the painstaking efforts put in by Brigadier Nilendra Kumar in producing this useful and thought provoking book.

(VP Malik)
General

Preview

It gives me great pleasure to write this preview to Brig. Nilendra Kumar's book. The book will be of great use to all those interested in military law. This publication provides a thorough overview of Military Law. It is not, however, a treatise that merely describes the law. It points the way ahead. It is an agenda for change. The author takes advantage of his considerable experience to highlight many of the practical infirmities in the law.

Chapter one outlines a system of ethics for personnel conducting court martial. They consist of rules that prescribe the behaviour of officers that will allow them to maintain impartiality. Chapter Two sets out the recent procedural amendments to Military Law. It also provides a very brief overview of the scope of Military Law. These amendments are said to have been made in the interest of fair play and human rights. The author considers the amendment that mandates speaking orders for Court Martial. It is surprising to note that such a provision did not exist until recently. The author concludes that more amendments are necessary to ensure that Military Law is in harmony with the law of the land. Chapter Three deals with the provisions relating to imprisonment under the Army Regulations. The author has compared the conditions that exist in a civilian prison with that of a military prison. Conditions in the prisoners rights cases should also be extended to military imprisonment. An example is the need for the introduction of a parole system under the Army Act. Chapter Four deals with the subject of charges. The author provides a thumbnail sketch of the various issues that must be kept in mind when the charge is being framed. He deals specifically with the issue of alternative charges; the charges ought not be conflicting, the officer incharge must examine the charges carefully to see that there is no real conflict. Chapter Five deals with the issue of apeals from Court Martial; specifically, Sections 164 and 179 of the Army Act are analysed. The author clarifies the underlying conflict in these provisions. This provision has been held to apply only to people still in the Army, the benefits do not extend to people who have retired or have been discharged. This means that people who are no longer in the Army cannot appeal. This seems unfair. The author suggests some remedies here. Chapter Six deals with appeals against a Court Martial. The author mentions that the law as it existed allowed only those still in the Army to take advantage of the appeals under the Act. This position has changed and now appeals are allowed even by those who have retired. He then examines the true scope and ambit of these provisions. In Chapter Seven the author charts the future course of military law. He suggests that there should be a services tribunal to handle all courts martial and other grievances that may be there. He also proposes a judicial service within the army to man these tribunals. He also suggests computerization of all the records of the Army as well as provision for counselling. In Chapter Eight the author looks at the various problems that plague the Indian legal system and suggests changes. In Chapter Nine the author looks at the relationship between human rights and Military Law. In this context, he looks at the power of arrest of Army officials. The author is of the view that this power is exercised quite indiscriminately in the Army. Confinement is usually solitary and all pay etc. is foregone. This the author holds is against the law laid down by the Supreme Court in the prisoners rights cases. He concludes that the provisions relating to arrest needs to reviewed. Chapter ten deals with the creation of proper mechanisms for the speady disposal of cases through the use of ADR methods. He specifies the various modes for dealing with different sorts of cases. In the last three chapters, the author deals with the problem of human rights and the Army.

The message of this work cannot be ignored. Military law has to be in conformity with the law of the land. The special needs of a fighting force cannot over-ride some of the basic principles of our legal system. A balance has to be struck between the demands of discipline in the Military and the fundamental rights of all individuals. The delicate balance cannot be achieved by abstract legal theory. Any change that is sought to be made must be the result of an understanding of legal principles as well as ground realities. This equilibrium has been admirably achieved by the author.

I recommend this book to anyone who is interested in Military Law as it exists but also in its future.

Prof. N. L. Mitra
Director
National Law School of India
University of Bangalore, Bangalore

Preface

There being no treatise on the theory and practice of Military Law, the entire law or the requirements of the law hardly, if ever, come to the notice of its users. Articles on issues of relevance to Military Law are not readily available to the students, teachers, lawyers and the Armed Forces personnel. The present book is a collection of disparate articles which try to examine various situations, problems and issues concerning matters interwoven with military and legal provisions.

My earlier book *Law Relating to the Army in India* received patronising welcome from one and all and this encouraged me to take up work for this volume. The present exercise of discussing the relevant contours and substance of law relating to the Army is holistic in nature and probably is the first of its kind.

Having had over three decades of association with the uniform, I cherish a deep sense of dedication and devotion to the service. My objective in writing this book must not be misconstrued as an attempt to run down the organisation. On the contrary it is an humble attempt to carry out a detailed appraisal of the existing scene and to suggest some well intentioned steps to further improve the system.

A few words about the aim and scope of the articles chosen for inclusion in this book. Service tribunals have been invested with wide powers over the personal liberty and career of delinquents brought to trial before them. "Professional Conduct Expected from Officers Handling Disciplinary Cases in the Army", portrays a code of ethics for such officers operating in a quasi-judicial capacity. A few humanitarian aspects have been highlighted in the articles "Recent Changes made to Army Act and Rules" and "Futuristic Trends in Military Laws". Great hardship and misery is caused to service personnel when they are taken into military custody and against which they have no provisions to secure bail. "Legal Provisions Relating to Imprisonment Under Military Custody" is an attempt to discuss allied issues.

Hasty investigations in order to achieve quick results may lead to an undeserved acquittal. "Framing of Charges Under the Army Act" contains useful guidelines for the officers responsible to frame charge sheets against accused persons. The nature of evidence marshalled in different types of cases often demand that alternative charges be drafted. More often than not it is as a result of incomplete investigations and an aim to secure conviction of the accused on one charge or the other. "Record of Findings on Alternative Charges by the Court Martial" depicts the legal position for officers serving on courts martial while deliberating on their findings.

The scope of "In House Remedies Against Courts Martial Verdicts" needs to be suitably studied so as to derive optimum use therefrom by the military men rather than rushing to civil courts. "Management of Indian Legal System and Reforms in Judiciary" is a collation of random thoughts motivated primarily with the desire to suggest changes in the judicial process so as to help and benefit a common man in his quest for justice. "Human Rights and Handling of

Disciplinary Cases in the Army" is an attempt to probe the basic processes governing the military system which was devised to obtain a high standard of discipline from its subjects.

Army wives have an important role to play in the career of their husbands and children. Imparting of basic knowledge to them in the matters of relevance has been discussed in "Legal Awareness for Army Wives". The problem arising from a large number of pending disciplinary and legal cases prompted working out modalities to devise means for their settlement. The same has been discussed in "Alternative Disputes Redressal for Speedy Disposal of Court Cases Pertaining to Armed Forces". Education is what survives when what has been learnt has been long forgotten. "Role of the Army Educational Corps in the 21st Century" makes an attempt to redefine the role of this Corps.

Military decision makes ought not to overlook the legally binding nature of International Humanitarian Law (IHL) applicable in armed struggles, (i.e. the law of war). The Armed Forces are the first to be concerned with and responsible for the implementation of the rules prescribed for armed conflicts. The articles "IHL: Perspective and Challenges in 21st Century" and "IHL in the Context of Wars of National Liberation" are the author's view point with regard to two specific issues concerning IHL. The contents and scope of the last article related to "Military Law Approach to the prosecution for the violations of International Humanatarian Law."

Some of these articles had already appeared in service and law journals. An attempt was made to update and revise them before inclusion in this work. The case law discussed in this book is as it stood on 13 July 1998. This book is intended to be of some help to all those connected with Military Law. It will also be found to be of considerable use to the decision makers and by those who, though well versed in Military Science, are called upon to discharge duties connected with legal and disciplinary cases. I hope the book will be found of some use even by the members of the Bar who will find in it a gist of the case law which has relevance to the topics under discussion.

I am extremely thankful to General V P Malik, PVSM, AVSM, ADC, Chief of the Army Staff and Chairman, Chief of Staff Committee who has written the Foreword. I am also obliged to Prof. N L Mitra, Director, National Law School of India University, Bangalore, for writing the preview for this book. I express my deep gratitude to my old friend and course-mate Lt Col A J Arul Raj (Retd), the renowned cartoonist, who in his own way has contributed to the overall get up of the work by drawing illustrations. My thanks also go to my colleague Major Mohd Yaseen who readily agreed to do a few cartoons for the books. I owe a special debt of thanks to my wife Rekha for enthusing me to complete this work in a record time. This work would have taken much more time to conclude but for the help rendered by my friend M A Paul in typing out the manuscript meticulously. Lastly, I place on record my special thanks to my Publishers for seeing the book through the Press.

I would look upon the constructive criticism of my readers with gratitude as such inter-action would ultimately enhance the aims and utility of this book as also future works.

Brig. Nilendra Kumar

Contents

Table of Cases

All India Bank Employees Assn. V National Industrial Tribunal; AIR 1962 SC 171.

Balwinder Kaur V UOI; Punjab & Haryana High Court CWP No 9759 of 1993.

Bhuvan Mohan Patnaik V State of AP; AIR 1974 SC 2092

Bhuwneshwar Singh, Sep V UOI; 1993 Cri LJ 3454 (SC)

C Ravichandran Iyer V Justice A M Bhattacharjee;1995SC(Cri) 953.

C S Rao V The Supreme Commander, AIR 1980, Andhra 172.

Charanjit Kaur V UOI; AIR 1994 SC 1491

Chúnoo V State; AIR 1954 All 795.

D B Mohan Patnaik V State of UP; (1975) 3 SCC 185.

Delhi Domestic Working Women's Forum V UOI; 1995 SCC(Cri) 7.

Dhingra HC, Lt Col (TS) V UOI; 1988(2) Delhi Lawyer(DB) 109.

Francis Coralie Mullin V Delhi Admn; (1981) 1 SCC 608.

Gian Chand V UOI; 1983 Cri LJ 1059 (Delhi).

Girija Barua, Smt V UOI; 1993(1) Gauhati Law Journal 169.

Gopinathan, Maj V UOI; AIR 1963 MP 249, 1963 (2) Cri L J 161.

Gurdip Kaur V UOI; Punjab & Haryana High Court CWP No 7539 of 1993.

H K Dalmia V Delhi Admn; AIR 1962 SC 1821

Harish Uppal, Capt V UOI; Supreme Court SLP No 5087 of 1984.

Jolly George Verghese and another V Bank of Cochin, AIR 1980 SC 470.

Kameshwar V State; AIR 1958 All 319.

Kartar Singh V State of Punjab; 1994 Cri LJ 3139.

Kishore Singh Ravinder Dev V State of Rajasthan;AIR 1981 SC 625.

Khatri V State of Bihar; AIR 1981 SC 928.

Krishnan Balakrishnan V State of Kerala ; AIR 1958 KER 94

L Chandra Kumar V UOI; Supreme Court CA No.481 of 1989.

LIC V Manubhai, AIR 1993 SC 171.

M Ramnarain (P) Ltd. V STC; AIR 1983 SC 786.

Madhu Kishwar V State of Bihar; (1996) 5 SCC 125.

Maharashtra Board V K S Gandhi; (1991) 2 SCC 716.

M A Rajasekhar V State of Karnataka; (1996) 10 SCC 369.

Manjit Singh, Ex. Sepoy V UOI; Punjab & Haryana Cri Misc. Petition No 17437 of 1994.

Mt. Choki V State; AIR 1957 Raj 11.

Mulkh Raj V UOI; 1983 Cri LJ 1794 (J&K).

Munna Lal Khatik V State ; AIR 1967 Cal 478.

Naga People's Movement of Human Rights V UOI, Supreme Court W P (Criminal) No. 550 of 1982.

Nargesh Meerza V IAC; 1981 (2) SLJ 349(SC).

Nutan Arvind V UOI; (1996) 2 SCC 488.

Rev Mons SFXDR Monterio V State of Goa; AIR 1970 SC 329.

R Shanmugain V OC 65 Coy ASC; 1984 (1) SLR 109.

Ranjit Thakur V UOI; AIR 1987 SC 2386.

S N Mukherjee V UOI; 1990 Cri LJ 2148 (SC), 1991 SLJ 1 (SL).

S Ramachandra Raju V State of Orissa; (1994) 5 SLR 199.

S Rangarajan V P Jagjivan Ram;(1989) 2 SCC 574,(1989)2 SCJ 128.

Sachidanand Pandey V State of WB; AIR 1987 SC 1109.

Sanjiv Datta's case; 1995 Cri LJ 2910 (SC).

Santokh Singh V Delhi Admn; AIR 1973 SC 1091.

Sharma JC V UOI; 1985 Cri LJ 696 (Him).

Sidhu KNS, Lt Col V UOI; 1977 (2) SLR 479 (Punj & Har).

Siemens Engineering & Manufacturing Co V UOI;AIR1976SC 1785.

Sodhi G S, Maj V UOI; Supreme Court WP (Cri) No 478 of 1989; AIR 1981 SC 1617.

State of Haryana V P C Wadhwa; AIR 1987 SC 1201.

State of J&K V J&K High Court Bar Assn; 1994 Supp(3)SCC 708.

Sukha V State of Rajasthan; AIR 1956 SC 513.

Sunil Bawa, Lt Col V UOI; 1994 (8) SLR 253 (MP).

Suraj Pal V State of UP; AIR 1955 SC 419.

UOI V Anand Singh Bisht; 1996 SCC (Cri) 1198.

UOI V Brigadier J S Sivia, Supreme Court Civil Appeal No. 1321 of 1991.

Willie Stanley V State of MP; 1956 Cri LJ 302 (SC).

Yusuf Abdul Aziz V State of Bombay; 1954 SCR 930.

Abbreviations

AEC	Army Educational Corps
Admn	Administration
AIR	All India Reporter
AISLJ	All India Services Law Journal
ADR	Alternative Disputes Redressal
AWWA	Army Wives Welfare Association
Bomb L.R.	Bombay Law Reporter
CDA	Controller of Defence Accounts
CO	Commanding Officer
Cri LJ	Criminal Law Journal
CR	Confidential Report
CrPC	Criminal Procedure Code
CSD	Canteen Stores Dept
ICRC	International Committee of the Red Cross
GCM	General Court Martial

IHL	International Humanitarian Law
HRD	Human Resources Development
IML	Institute of Military Law
JAG	Judge Advocate General
JCO	Junior Commissioned Officer
NDA	National Defence Academy
NCO	Non Commissioned Officer
OTA	Officers Training Academy
RI	Rigorous Imprisonment
SCC	Supreme Court Cases
SCM	Summary Court Martial
Sec	Section
Sep	Sepoy
SLJ	Services Law Journal
SLR	Services Law Reporter
Supdt	Superintendent
TADA	Terrorist & Disruptive Activities (Prevention) Act
UEI	Unit Education Instructor
UOI	Union of India
WA	Writ Appeal
WP	Writ Petition

1

Professional Conduct Expected from Officers Handling Disciplinary Cases in the Army

> "I shall strive till I eradicate impiety and injustice and till I establish a rule of justice and truth, a humane and heavenly regime".
>
> Nahzul Balagha, Sermon 38

Every profession has its own ethics. It is the code of honour of professional conduct which distinguishes a profession from a mere occupation. The attitude, conduct and behaviour of various officials performing quasi judicial functions in the armed forces is expected to be at the same pedestal as the standards expected from the civil judiciary. This is so because they are entrusted with matters that decide liberty or future course of service career of other servicemen. Any laxity in their conduct may have serious repurcussion on the discipline of the armed forces. Discipline is what sets apart a soldier from a dacoit. However, there are no written guidelines available on this matter with the units and formations. An attempt has been made in this article to discuss the relevance of this issue.

Noted Jurist V R Krishna Iyer had once remarked, "We expect judicial dignity and decorum, becoming comily in public and projection of an institutional image which inspires confidence in the people that public justice is in their solemn keeping".

The Supreme Court had indicated its mind clearly in the case of C Ravichandran Iyer V Justice A M Bhattacharjee; 1995 SCC (Cri) 953 when it held that "Society is entitled to expect that a Judge must be a man of high integrity, honesty, and required to have moral vigour, ethical firmness and, impervious to corrupt or venia! influences. Even his private life must adhere to high standards of probity and propriety higher than those deemed acceptable to others. Therefore, the Judge can ill afford to seek shelter from the fallen standards in the society". There are various stages when the above dicta needs to be scrupulously adhered to by the military superiors.

Let us first take the case of the Commanding Officer of a unit. He is one of the most important officials armed with the powers to deal with disciplinary cases. Although he cannot award punishment to an officer, he is empowered with the requisite authority to dispose off cases in respect of Junior Commissioned Officers and other ranks. He is vested with suitable powers to summarily deal with their cases under Army Act Sections 80, 85 and constitutes Summary Court Martials combining in him the dual role of a judge and prosecutor. In the case of officers, he himself carries out hearing of charge and orders recording of summary of evidence. At an appropriate stage of a case he issues charge sheets and remands the accused for trial by court martial.

Fair and Impartial

In view of his onerous role, it is essential that his conduct should be entirely fair and above board. An officer

The 'SUM'-ing up
PROSECUTION WITNESSES + CONFESSIONAL STATEMENTS × DIRECT EVIDENCE − DEFENCE WITNESSES ÷ IAFD 905 =
IT'S AMAZING! HE HAS MADE THE ENTIRE CASE LOOK SO SIMPLE.
YASEEN

I OBJECT TO THIS, YOUR HONOUR! THE DEFENDING OFFICER HAS GONE TOO FAR, IN INTERPRETING THE TERM - "CROSS" - EXAMINATION.
PROSECUTION WITNESS
PROSECUTOR
DEFENDING OFFICER
YASEEN

discharging judicial functions must be impartial. He must not have the slightest interest in the result or outcome of the case. He should not be biased in favour of the prosecution more than the defence. His attitude towards the case should be indifferent and unprejudiced. Freedom from bias on his part should be clearly discernable. Such a person should extend to the accused the humane presumptions of the law and keep his mind in such condition with reference to the accused that guilt must be affirmatively and conclusively shown before he is willing to convict.

What is bias? It indicates a leaning of the mind and prepossession. It sways the mind towards one opinion rather than another and thereby influences the judgement. Any conduct which shows that the authority cannot act with an open mind or that he would decide a case otherwise than on evidence would constitute bias. Bias in context of military tribunals was discussed by the Supreme Court in the case of Ranjit Thakur V UOI; AIR 1987 SC 2387. The Apex Court held that, "it is the essence of a judgement that it is made after due observance of the judicial process, that the court or tribunal passing it observe at least the minimal requirements of natural justice and is composed of impartial persons acting fairly and without bias and in good faith. What is relevant is the reasonableness of the apprehension in that regard in the mind of the party. The proper approach for the Judge is not to look at his own mind and ask himself however honestly, "Am I biased?" but to look at the mind of the party before him".

"Bias" is not synonymous with "prejudice". A man cannot be prejudiced against another, without being biased against him, but he may be biased without being prejudiced. It is of essence in judicial matters that the authority making decisions should be able to act impartially, objectively and without any bias. This principle is violated when such an authority is himself personally interested in the case before him

The above principles demand that a Commanding Officer should deliberately avoid any intimacy with the accused or display any bias against him. Where the accused is of the rank of an officer, the Commanding Officer must take care to avoid any social interaction with him to the extent possible. For example, where the accused is an officer belonging to the same unit and the Commanding Officer attends a lavish feast at his house, then surely such a conduct cannot but be characterised as improper on his part. It would also not be in order for a Commanding Officer to accept from the accused, directly or indirectly, any gift or present which can be said to cast a shadow of doubt on his impartiality.

It is not the accused alone with regard to whom the professional conduct of the Commanding Officer has to be above board. He must not show any favour or affection towards witnesses for the prosecution. Otherwise it may tend to give an impression that he is trying to "fix" the accused. Needless to say the Commanding Officer is duty bound to be sympathetic to the accused to the extent that the offender is also an army personal and as such 'Comrade in arms'. Therefore, there can be no objection if he is rightly concerned about the welfare of the delinquent. Such a welfare may, for example, mean that the genuine requirements of the family members of the accused need to be taken care of.

Favour or Partiality

A cardinal principle of criminal jurisprudence stipulates that the accused is presumed to be innocent till proven guilty. Further, it is not upon him to prove his innocence. To translate this dictum into practice, in the arena of military justice, the approach and conduct of the Commanding Officer should be absolutely above board. He must not accept any favour from or show partiality to the accused. He must not exhibit any bias against him.

There should be no occasion for a superior to show callous indifference and insensitivity to his mandatory duties which affect the basic rights of an accused. A derogatory or contemptuous remark or hostile comment made by the superior may be adequate to indicate his antagonism towards the person in the dock. An accused should not be treated as a social outcast. Even when placed under arrest the normal facilities to him and his family for private mail, drawal of canteen stores, ration and leave travel concession etc.,should be provided uninterrupted. In particular requirements of medical help to him and his family should not be denied. Similarly, genuine needs for transport should be met specially in far away cantonments devoid of public transportation.

The accused should not be unnecessarily kept under detention. Desirability to review the mode of arrest should be suitably examined at regular intervals.

Discriminatory treatment to the prosecution and defence witnesses should be avoided. It would be improper for the Commanding Officer to express any opinion with regard to the outcome of the trial or conviction of the accused.

In the similar manner the attitude and approach of the members of the court martial is required to be same as that discussed above. Courts martial are tribunals composed under the statutory powers to try an offender on a charge sheet. It would be pertinent to reproduce the views of the Supreme Court while a three judges bench expressed displeasure at the attitude of a Chief Election Commissioner. The Apex Court remarked "all those who hold high constitutional offices should not think it their private property. If they do so, they will only be harming the credibility of the office they hold".

The members of the court martial should be careful about their personal conduct. There should be no display of emotion or sentiment. "A judge neither rewards virtue nor chastises vice. He only administers even handed justice between man and man even between the citizen and the State". Sentiment is a dangerous will-o'-the -wisp to take as a guide in the search for legal principles. A member must decide the case on legal evidence and not allow himself to be carried away by his sympathy for either party. His language should be sober and temperate and in no case satirical or factious. He should be dignified and restrained in the expression of his opinion. The members should not appear to be at daggers drawn amongst themselves. According to a famous jurist, "The Judges, at the higher echelons, may like their little persons, perhaps, squabble privately, denounce in secrecy and even criticise mutually intramurally. But beyond that point lead to a crisis where a code of conduct may be needed to discipline them into high behaviour"

Command Influence

In so far as the convening authority is concerned, while assembling the court and deciding the composition of the court martial, it must not give any signal which can tantamount to exerting any "command influence". It would be improper that he forces the weight of his military command upon the officers chosen from amongst his subordinates to serve as members upon the court martial. A warrant holder must not under any occasion address the members of the court, whether individually or collectively, about the merits of the case. He must not express any comment about the final outcome of the trial.

There is a settled tradition governing the discharge of the judicial function that while an officer is seized of a judicial or quasi-judicial matter then even the highest officer above him should not give him any advice or talk over the matter with him. Such a tradition deserves to be strictly followed.

A few salient points need to be included in the code of ethics which should be drawn up in detail for the members of the court and the Judge Advocate. The same could go to form the guidelines of the professional conduct expected from the members of the Court Martial. These could state that the members must not favour or condemn an accused because of the emotions of the human mind, heart or affections. They must act only on the evidence and arguments put forth before them and not on any information which they receive from the outside. Every member should be wholly free from even the suspicion of bias. The accused, should not, must not be pre-judged.

During the course of the trial, the interaction between the court and the convening authority should avoid any reference to the merits of the case. It was opined by the eminent legal authority G S Pathak, "A Judge cannot preserve justice for the Common Man, unless he is independent of the executive for he decides not only between man and man, but also between an individual and the community and the individual and the State itself".

Circulars have been issued in the past laying down that during the course of a trial the Judge Advocate should not share accommodation or transport with the prosecutor or any of the prosecution witnesses. The members of the court and the Judge Advocate, should, to the extent practicable, avoid any social inter course with the prosecution witnesses or the accused. Judge Advocate should not engage in a conversation with the prosecutor alone. He must make it a point always to talk to him within hearing distances of the defence counsel and the defending officer.

The efficacy of the courts martial to maintain discipline in the armed forces can exist only so long as their verdicts are perceived as just and fair. Any trace of bias, partiality or malafide act on their part would erode the faith and confidence of the troops in such a judicial system.

2

Recent Changes Made in Military Law

"Too much legislative activity is as harmful as too little".

Justice M Hidayatullah

The armed forces are governed by the provisions of the Army Act 1950 (Act XLVI of 1950) which was specially enacted to cater for the peculiar working conditions of the men in uniform and analogous enactments. The Army Act in its present form came into force on 22 July 1950. It is patterned on the model of Indian Army Act that was applicable to the troops of the Indian Army prior to the independence.

While on one hand the soldiers are governed by the Army Act, on the other they are also subject to other prevailing laws of the land. Therefore, a soldier who commits any civil offence is deemed to be guilty of an offence under the Army Act and is liable to be tried by a court martial and on conviction may be punished accordingly.

Certain procedural safeguards have been made available to all ranks of the Army for seeking in house redressal of their grievances relating to service. Further, these persons are not debarred from approaching the Supreme Court or various

High Courts with prayer for judicial review in case they feel aggrieved. The provisions of the Army Act, other rules and service regulations have been frequently put to critical judicial scrutiny during the passage of last five decades. Decisions in these cases as also the increased emphasis to human rights have led to a number of major changes introduced in last four or five years to the Army Act and the Army Rules.

The disciplinary process against an accused in the Army starts with the hearing of charge which entails preliminary investigation. According to the earlier procedure the hearing of charges was not obligatory in the case of officers and it was carried out in his presence only when he so demanded it. Under the amended rules, the procedure for hearing of charge for all accused persons has been made similar irrespective of their rank. Hence, there is no disparity in the manner of investigation of charges whether the accused be an officer or a plain sepoy.

A few significant changes have been made to cut down delay in the disposal of cases. Primarily such measures are designed to speed up the investigation of charges and the procedures at the pre- trial stages. One of the major changes introduced stipulates that if an incident had been earlier investigated by a court of inquiry where the delinquent was afforded opportunity to defend his character and military reputation, then at the commencement of the disciplinary process the subsequent hearing of charge may be dispensed with. The aim of such an amendment is to cut down duplication of efforts and consequential delay. Further, in case the evidence, which has been reduced to writing, discloses an offence different than the one on which preliminary investigation was conducted, then the case may proceed on the basis of fresh evidence. The authorities thereby need not go back to the stage of hearing of charge to hear the charge afresh.

For example, the preliminary investigation in the case of an accused could have been held for a lapse relating to loss of an item of government property by neglect whereas the evidence when reduced to writing may indicate dishonest misappropriation. The offender may then be brought to trial for the latter offence. This change too would obviously effect considerable saving in time.

To provide utmost latitude to the defence, the amended Rules now lay down that it would invariably be the prosecution side who would be required to put forth their arguments after the examination of witnesses is concluded. Thereby the defence/accused would always get an opportunity to give his reply which was not the case earlier.

Speaking Orders

Undoubtedly one of the most radical changes introduced pertains to speaking orders. So far the courts martial were not required to spell out the reasons in support of the findings recorded by them. In fact such practice existed in almost all the systems where jury trial is in vogue. However, according to the latest amendments, every General or District Court Martial would be required to record brief reasons to justify their findings on each charge. Consequent to this change, the records of the courts martial will clearly reveal a gist of the factual details and legal issues which influenced the minds of the members of the courts martial to arrive at a particular decision. Accordingly, the scope for arbitrary decisions and non-application of mind by the court members has been reduced. Moreover, the confirming authority will be consequently in a better position to evaluate the analysis of evidence recorded at the trial.

General and Summary General Courts Martial are empowered to award death penalty where it is so provided for the offence charged. The Rules now stipulate that before confirming the sentence of death, the accused person shall be duly explained his rights to present a petition against the proposed punishment.

It was experienced that considerable time was spent at the investigating stage in procuring attendance of civil witnesses. It was felt that the relevant provisions of the Act had become out of date and insufficient for modern day requirement where often testimony of civilian witnesses appears to be relevant. At times immediately after their retirement army personnel used to avoid appearing before courts of inquiry on the plea that they were not subject to the Army Act any more. To give more teeth to the investigating process, the courts of inquiry have now been invested with statutory powers to summon civilian witnesses.

One of the welcome changes pertains to doing away with field punishments. Since the days of the East India Company it was not uncommon for courts martial to order a delinquent to undergo field punishment. Such a sentence was only awarded to the NCOs and soldiers on active duties. It could not be inflicted on an officer. This punishment usually entailed keeping the convict under fetters and handcuffs to prevent his escape after getting him tied to a fixed object. Irons and ropes were used for tying the convicts. This punishment was considered very harsh and had rarely been put to use in last few decades. The recent amendments have deleted the provisions of field punishment from the statutes.

Period of Limitation

There was a feeling that the Commanding Officers (COs) were powerless to deal with the JCOs. To make the institution of COs more effective they are now empowered to decide cases of JCOs and award them punishment upto 'Severe Reprimand'. However, this power can only be put to use by a CO holding the rank of a Colonel.

SAAB! THERE WAS A 'MAJOR BREAK-THROUGH' IN THE OPERATION.
NONSENSE! WHY 'MAJOR' SAAB GOT 'BREAK-THROUGH', INFACT THERE SHOULD HAVE BEEN NO CASUALTY AT ALL.
YASEEN

NEVER KNEW! ADVERTISEMENT WILL MAKE IT'S PRESENCE HERE ALSO.
COURT MARTIAL SPONSORED BY
(1) PROSECUTION WITNESSES - PROCTOR & GABLE
(2) DEFENCE WITNESSES - DETTOL
(3) COURT WITNESSES - CIBA GAIGY
COURT MARTIAL
YASEEN

It was long felt that the period of limitation for trial by courts martial frequently came in the way of initiating disciplinary process. The original provision had fixed the time limit of three years for commencement of trial from the date of offence. A feeling of helplessness existed because such period of limitation stood in the way of action against delinquents whose charges came to surface at a later stage. The problem was being felt after the law laid down consequent upon the decision of Delhi High Court in the case of Lt Col H C Dhingra; 1988 (2) Delhi Lawyers (DB) 109 where the Court had viewed Section 122 (1) as an absolute bar, "It is a prohibitory provision. No provision has been made for extension of the time prescribed by it. The power of authorities under the Act to try any person for any offence, except as provided under Section (2) is restricted by statutory provision. This provision is not consensual. Its operation does not depend upon volition, will or consent of anyone. Its operation cannot be waived". As a result of the experience gained, an amendment was carried out and the new Section 122 which provides that this period shall be computed from the date of offence or when the offence comes to surface or when the identity of the offender gets known.

In the earlier scheme of the Statute a person who had retired from army service could be brought to trial for any lapse done by him while in service. The only condition imposed was that the trial was required to commence within six months from the date of his retirement. In some cases this time span was found to be inadequate to proceed against offenders whose lapses came to be known after a few months and the investigations could not be completed within the limit of six months. This time has been extended to three years and does not include the period when the offender absconds to evade his arrest or secures a stay order from a court.

Benefit of Set Off

With a view to reduce and mitigate pre trial hardships of the accused persons, Section 169 has been given a new shape to provide that the period spent by an accused in civil or military custody awaiting trial be excluded from the term of imprisonment awarded by a court martial. The amended section now is in tune with the provisions of Section 428 of Cr PC. In an indirect appreciation of such an amendement, the Supreme Court, in the case of Union of India V Anand Singh Bisht; 1996 SCC (Cri) 1198; proceeded to suggest that it would be desirable that a provision regarding set-off similar to Section 169-A of the Army Act and a provision similar to Army Rule 27 should be incorporated in the Border Security Force Act, 1968 and the Rules. As of present, the benefit of Set-off of period of detention undergone during investigation, inquiry or trial against sentence of imprisonment is not available to a person belonging to the Border Security Force.

To cut down delay in processing of requests for maintenance to be awarded to the wives and children, the prescribed authority has been now entrusted to the Chief of the Army Staff or an Army Commander in the case of officers as against the Central Government as prescribed earlier. The amendment made to Army Rule 193 has thus simplified the procedure for grant of maintenance to some extent.

All these modifications have been done according to the requirements of time and need for streamlining the process of dispensation of justice. However, these changes alone are not adequate. Further progressive amendements are required to be made in Army Law to be in consonance with the law of the land as also requirements of military discipline.

3

Legal Provisions Relating to Imprisonment under Military Custody

> "In our world prisons are still laboratories of torture, warehouses in which human commodities are sadistically kept and where spectrum of inmates range from drift-wood juveniles to heroic dissenters".
>
> Justice V R Krishna Iyer

The National Human Rights Commission has drawn the attention of the Government to the poor conditions prevailing in jails and asked the Government to ensure the enactment of uniform and consolidated law on prisons for the entire country. It has pointed out that the provisions of 102 year old Prison Act are totally outdated to cater to the modern requirement of purposeful custody, reformation and treatment of prisoners.

Army personnel are governed by the self contained code enacted as the Army Act. The statute provides different provisions that regulate award of imprisonment to the persons subject to the Military Law after having been pronounced guilty of offences listed in the Act.

One of the effective tools available with a commanding officer to maintain discipline in his unit is the authority entrusted to him whereby he can bring an offender to trial by Summary Court Martial (SCM) or dispose off his case by way of summary trial under section 80 of the Army Act. In the case of former, he is armed with the powers to award imprisonment upto one year whereas in the other option such power is limited to 28 days imprisonment.

In the case of SCM, imprisonment could be carried out in military custody or in a civil prison which is required to be recorded in the commital warrant. On the other hand, the imprisonment awarded under section 80 is to be undergone in the military custody. Substantive law in this regard is contained in Army Act sections 167, 169 (3), 170, 172 and Army Rule 168 (2). Imprisonment in military custody is required to be carried out in the Quarterguard or cell of a unit.

Army Act Sec 169 (3) provides that in the case of a sentence of imprisonment for a period not exceeding three months and passed under the Army Act by a court martial, the appropriate officer may direct that the sentence shall be carried out by confinement in military custody. A guideline has been provided under Note 2 to the ibid section which says that such sentences to which no sentence of dismissal has been added should be carried out by confinement in military custody. Usually, the prisoners for whom it would be desirable to be retained in military service after completion of their imprisonment term are sent to military custody to undergo their punishment.

Subjection to Military Law while in Custody

Army Rule 168(2) stipulates that when dismissal is combined with imprisonment which is to be carried out in military custody, the dismissal shall not take effect until the date on which the prisoner is released from military custody. Put simply what it means is that a convict shall continue to remain subject to the Army Act while undergoing his term of imprisonment.

It is not only the prisoners who are awarded imprisonment to be undergone in military custody who are kept under such custody. Vide Regulaltions for the Army para 495, any prisoner under sentence of imprisonment may properly be held in military custody pending his despatch to a civil or military prison. Thus, during active operations or while arrangements are being made for the despatch of a convict to a civil jail or military prison, he is kept confined in the military custody.

It would be interesting to make a comparable study of the provisions governing holding in custody as applicable to civilian inmates with those in military quarterguard cells. A convict undergoing imprisonment in a civil jail is entitled to apply for leave or parole. The jail manual provides for the same. On the contrary, no such provision exists under the Army Regulations for the prisoners undergoing imprisonment in military custody. The entitlement of an accused convicted by a court martial to seek parole for specific purposes such as death or serious illness of a close relation and for treatment of important diseases were conceded to by the Punjab & Haryana High Court in the case Ex-Sepoy Manjit Singh V UOI; Cri Misc Petition No 17437 of 1994.

Mode of Captivity

Regulations for the Army contain a few provisions to regulate the mode of implementation of imprisonment. It provides that "all prisoners will be visited daily by the orderly officer. They will also be visited by the officer of the week." However, instructions should be drafted to clearly explain as to what is the duty of the officers undertaking such visits. It would be desirable to incorporate suitable provisions about rendition of medical aid to the inmates of the cell and about their access to a medical officer. This could be done at the commencement and termination of custody or otherwise when so required.

It is also provided that such prisoners will be confined separately in the quarter guard or cell as far as possible and in no case will two prisoners be confined in the same cell. They will always be under the observation of a sentry. If a prisoner is admitted in hospital, a sentry may be posted over him. Such provisions are self explanatory and there can be no dispute about need for suitable measures to ensure security of the prisoners. It was held by the Supreme Court in Bhuvan Mohan Patnaik V State of AP; AIR 1974 SC 2092 that, "whatever be the nature and extent of the petitoner's fundamental right to life and personal liberty they have no fundamental right to escape from lawlful custody".

What is to be the daily routine of the prisoners ? Regulation para 509 lays down that they would be required to work for six hours daily from mid March to mid October and seven hours daily from mid October to mid March. The work will comprise military instructions for minimum two hours daily and hard labour for remaining duration. It is to consist of labour tasks such as spade work and working parties but no task will exceed a period of two hours at a time. In the hot season, hard labour will be performed under cover.

Liberal changes have been brought in the prison administration and jail reforms introduced on the civil side. The Supreme Court has upheld the dignity of a person who is behind bars. Justice Chandrachud (as he then was) observed in DB Mohan Patnaik V State of UP; (1975) 3 SCC 185, "Convicts are not, by mere reason of the conviction, denuded of all the fundamental rights which they otherwise possess. A compulsion under the authority of law, following upon a conviction, to live in a prison house entails by its own force the deprivation of fundamental freedom like the right to move freely throughout the territory of India or right to practice a profession. But the Constitution guarantees other freedoms. Even a convict is entitled to some precious rights guaranteed by Article 21 that he should not be deprived of life or personal liberty except according to procedure established by law". Law on military side should keep pace with modern legal thinking so that such improvements may also be introduced for the persons being held in military custody.

Jail Reforms

A court curtails the freedom of a convict but does not take away his right to proper health. He should be allowed to take proper exercises and proper medical aid, when so required. Regulatory provisions need to be put forth to provide for issue of hot meals to the inmates. They should be entitled to receive visitors, relations and private mail. In Francis Coralie Mullin V Delhi Administration (1981) 1 SCC 608; Justice Bhagwati had observed, "personal liberty would include the right to socialise with members of the family and friends, subject of course, to any valid prison regulations". It was further held that the prison regulations imposing restrictions must be fair, reasonable and just. Justice Bhagwati was of the view that a detenue must be permitted to have at least two interviews in a week with relatives or friends, at any reasonable hour after obtaining prior permission from the Suprintendent of the Jail. Permission of any other authority was not necessary. Regulations for the Army have yet to introduce such facilities for men under detention.

While under custody, the offender forfeits all his pay and allowances. Vide Army Act Section 91 (a), deductions are mandatory of all pay and allowances for every day of such imprisonment. While this may also be the case with a civil servant but at least he gets paid for due work executed by him in the prison. That is not so for a person detained in military custody. On one hand, he does not get the pay and allowances which stand forfeited and on the other he does not get paid for the work he is made to do. It is for consideration that rather than being made to do fatigue, they should be directed to do some purposeful and constructive work and paid for the same.

It is not uncommon these days for army personnel holding graduate or post-graduate qualifications who come to be punished for some or the other lapse on their part. If detained in a civil prison they could have been entitled to a higher class vis Class B. However in the quarter guard cells there are no such facilities for higher class.

The convicts lodged in civil prisons are visited and their conditions ascertained by the officials of the Crime Prevention Society and other jail visitors. Attempts are made by such persons in all earnest to reform them. With some modifications such a reformative practice could also be adopted by the military system as well. A prisoner's stay in cell should be utilised to correct and reconstruct his future so that he comes out a better soldier and citizen.

Supreme Court has been very particular in safeguarding the plight of the prisoners. In the case of Sepoy Bhuwneshwar Singh V UOI; 1993 Cri LJ 3454 (SC), while enhancing the amount of compensation from Rs 1000 awarded by the High Court to Rs 30,000 for a delinquent subjected to three months illegal detention, the Supreme Court had held, "The payment of compensation in such cases is to be understood in the broader sense of providing relief by an order of making 'monetary amends' under the public law for the wrong done due to breach of public duty, of not protecting the fundamental rights of the citizen. The compensation is in the nature of the 'exemplary damages' awarded against the wrong doer for the breach of its public law duty". No doubt Army Act is designed to achieve a high standard of discipline and, therefore, action taken against defaulters should deter others. But humanitarian considerations do not deserve to be lost sight of. The words of TERENCE need to be remembered when he said that "Extreme law is often extreme injustice".

4

Framing of Charges under the Army Act

"Bread of deceit is sweet to a man; but afterwards his mouth shall be filled with gravel."

Proverbs 20 verse 17

A charge is a precise formulation of the specific accusation made against an accused person who is entitled to know its nature in clear language. It is imperative that the accusation is precisely and clearly formulated in writing. The whole object of framing a charge is to enable the accused to concentrate his attention to the accusation made against him so that he may be in a position to conduct his defence properly. If the charge is framed in such a manner that it does not clearly bring out the necessary ingredients of the offence then it becomes vague and defective.

According to the Rules of Procedure that were framed almost a century ago for the British Army, "The statement of the offence in each charge will be followed by the appropriate statement of particulars commencing with the words "in that he", etc or "in having", etc, and stating in brief ordinary language what the accused is alleged to have done." The above guideline is still valid.

In criminal prosecution, the framing of charges is carried out by the Magistrates or by the Public Prosecutors who are not only trained but also experienced in the task. However, in military units, framing of charge, in a large number of cases, is undertaken by the Commanding Officers who are not well versed in law or experienced to be in a position as aforesaid. Thereby the obvious need to exercise great care in drafting a charge sheet.

At what stage of the disciplinary process the charge sheet is prepared? It was held in the case of Gian Chand V UOI, 1983 Cri LJ 1059 (Delhi) that, "It is no doubt true that under sub rule (2) of Rule 28 it is stated that, a charge means an accusation contained in a charge sheet, but it must be borne in mind that the charge sheet is prepared only when the accused is required to be tried by a court martial. This stage arises after the summary of evidence had been recorded under Rule 23". Similarly, MP High Court had opined in the case of Major Gopinathan, AIR 1963 MP 249 that the framing of a charge is a step taken after investigation but before trial by court martial.

A charge sheet devoid of mistakes is a pre-requisite for a successful prosecution. The charge sheet, being the most essential document in the proceedings, should be free from corrections or erasures. On the other hand, the hard work put in, thorough investigations and the weight of solid evidence can be frustrated by a charge sheet containing mistakes in its contents.

The charge sheet should be specific and should contain the necessary particulars required by law. The exact details required such particulars, however, would depend upon the facts and circumstances of each case. The object in its formulation is that the accused is entitled to be informed with the greatest precision, what act or acts he is alleged to have committed and under what section of the code or other law infringed, they fall.

It was held by Calcutta High Court in the case of Munna Lal Khatik V State; AIR 1967 Cal 478 that charge is a first notice to the accused of his offence and should convey to him in sufficient clearness and certainty what the prosecution intends to prove against him and of which case the accused is to meet. "The framing of charge is vital to criminal trial and requires careful attention", as ruled in Krishnan Balakrishnan V State of Kerala, AIR 1958 KER 94.

The charge should avoid all unnecessary words. Abbreviations or recondite words should, as far as pososible be also not used. If the law which creates the offence does not give it any specific name, then definition of the offence must be stated so as to give the accused notice of the matter with which he is charged.

Explicit and Simple

All the essentials of an offence must be averred in a charge and as a whole. What is the yardstick to be applied to determine whether or not a charge ought to be held good ? The answer that if the head of the charge i.e. the statement of offence and the particulars taken together supply the court and the accused with sufficient information of the nature of the offence which the court has to try and an accused to defence, the charge ought to be held good. The validity of the charge must in each case be determined by the application of the test, viz., has the accused a reasonably sufficient notice of the matter with which he was charged.

In the framing of a charge, the language used should be explicit and simple. Each averment should be duly supported by evidence available. Care should be taken to ensure that under no circumstances should a charge suffer from any legal infirmity. Mistakes of law and language calling for intervention need to be attended to.

While framing charges, care must be taken to ensure that:

(a) the charges are simple,

(b) the particulars of the charge support the statement of offence,

(c) the charge must apprise the accused the precise accusation against him so that he knows what he is required to defend.

The first stipulation about a charge being simple means that it should be easy to understand. It should not be complicated. All unnecessary and irrelevant details must be excluded. But brevity should not be attempted at the cost of clarity.

With regard to the particulars of the charge it is important to meet the requirement to mention time and place of the alleged offence. The same would give reasonably sufficient notice to the accused of the matter with which he is charged. It is quite conveivable that in some cases by making a charge too vague in the matter of the time of the commission of the offence, an accused person may substantially be deprived of the opportunity to make a defence of alibi.

It is essential that the draft charge should be critically examined. If it is felt that the language used needs refinement and some unnecessary details are required to be deleted, then on reconsideration a revised draft charge sheet should be issued. However, it is not in all the cases that an error or ommission in the charge sheet deserves to be considered as material. The criterion in all such cases is firstly, whether the accused was actually misled by the error or omission and secondly, it resulted in failure of justice. To allow an error or omission in the charge to vitiate the entire trial, when the accused was not in any way misled or prejudiced thereby will be to allow technicality to prevail over justice and thereby defeat the very object for which the rules of procedure are framed.

Defects in Charge

It has already been said that the object of the charge is to give the accused notice of the matter he is charged with. Therefore any shortcoming does not touch upon jurisdiction at the trial. If the necessary information is conveyed to him and no prejudice is caused because of the charges, the accused cannot succeed by merely showing that the charges framed were defective. The Supreme Court had held in Willie Stanley V State of MP, 1956 Cri LJ 302 thus, "We are unable to find magic or charm in the ritual of a charge. It is the substance of these provisions (relating to charge) that count and not their outward form. To hold otherwise is only to provide avenues of escape for the guilty and afford no protection to the innocent".

The transactions that form the subject matter of the charge are not always simple and straight forward. What is to be done when an accused has committed more than one offence ? If, in one series of acts so connected together as to form the same transaction, more offences than one are committed by the same person, he may be charged with and tried at one trial for every such offence. The question then arises as to what is meant by "same transaction"? Where there is a proximity of time, or place, or unity of purpose and design, or continuity of action in respect of a series of acts, it may be possible to infer that they form part of the same transaction.

The real and substantial test for determining whether several offences are connected together so as to form one transaction depends upon whether they are so related to one another in point of purpose, or as cause and effect, or as principal and subsidiary acts so as to constitute one continuous action. It was held by Allahabad High Court in the case of Kameshwar V State; AIR 1958 All 318 that whether the series of acts are so connected as to form the same transaction would depend on the facts and circumstances of each case. In another case, it was held that in order to constitute one transaction there must be some continuity of purpose, Chunnoo V State; AIR 1954 All 798.

Same offences are said to be those offences which arise out of the same series of acts. Offences are considered to be of the same kind when they are punishable with the same amount of punishment under the same section of law.

It is wrong to frame more than one charge in respect of one and the same set of facts unless the additional charges are alternative. A separate charge, as required by the basic rules, is required to be framed for every distinct offence and not necessarily for "every" or "each" offence. Two offences are distinct if they are non-identical and are not in any way inter-related. Offences having no connection with each other are distinct offences. The decision of Allahabad High Court in the case of Chunnoo and others V State; AIR 1954 All 795 has put forth clear guidelines in this regard which are still valid. The Court held that, "the only meaning that the word "distinct" can have in the context in which it occurs is to indicate that there should be no connection between the various acts which give rise to criminal liability".

The framing of a specific and distinct charge is advisable in respect of every distinct head of criminal conviction and sentence therefor. In the case of Suraj Pal V State of UP; AIR 1995 SC 419, it was held that there can be no doubt that the direct individual liability of a person can only be fixed upon him with reference to a specific charge in respect of the particular offence. A "distinct" offence is distinguished from another offence by:

(a) Difference in time and/or place of their occurrence, or

(b) Victims of crime being different, or

(c) The acts constituting the offence are covered by different sections.

Infirmities in a Charge Sheet

There are various types of infirmities that may be noticed in a charge sheet. These may relate to a charge being badly framed or invalid or defective or bad or vague. It would be interesting to see as to when does a charge fall in any of the above category.

An omission, defect or error in the charge which does not prejudice or mislead the accused and does not result in any failure of justice cannot be regarded as material. In the question of prejudice the stage at which the objection is raised is material. If it is not raised till a late stage, no prejudice is to be inferred. The Supreme Court has held in the case of Sukha V State of Rajasthan; AIR 1956 SC 513, that, it will be slow to entertain question of prejudice when details are not furnished. The fact that the objection is not taken at an early stage will also be taken into account.

A charge can be said to be defective under certain contingencies such as:

(a) When particulars of the charge do not support the statement of offence, then the charge is said to be bad in law. When the statement of offence discloses an offence under the Army Act and one or more essential elements of that offence are omitted from the particulars then also the same defect emerges e.g. the omission of word "dishonestly" in a charge of "dishonestly misappropriating" would make it a bad charge.

(b) When two distinct and separate offences are included in one, the charge is said to be bad for duplicity. Such duplicity may be contained either in the statement of offence or in the particulars of the charge.

(c) The term "defective" when used in relation to a charge would mean that one of the necessary ingredients of the offence is not averred in its contents. At times, this is also used when there is a mistake in the name, rank or description of the accused or his unit. Defective charge, in that context, is to an extent, curable by the court.

(d) Invalid charge implies that all the essentials of an offence are not averred in a charge read as a whole. When the statement of offence is not supported by the particulars of the charge, it would be an invalid charge.

(e) A vague charge implies that the particulars of the charge do not specify any culpable act or omission but leave it to presumption. The Supreme Court had held in the case of H K Dalmia V Delhi Administration, AIR 1962 SC 1821; that vagueness of the charge would not make the trial illegal especially when no prejudice was caused to the accused.

The unnecessary multiplication of charges should be avoided. Such an error generally takes the form of preferring charges in respect of minor offences which accompany the principal offence, and are part of the same transaction, for example, a soldier gets drunk, uses violence to his superior officer accompanied by insubordinate language, and then resists the escort. Here a single charge for "using criminal force to superior officer" (and not four charges) will be enough. It has been held that absence of a proper charge is a material error which may be presumed to have misled the accused person in his defence and occasioned a failure of justice. What is the remedy ? In the absence of such a proper charge, retrial may be ordered.

Due care in formulation of charges is warranted at the pre-trial stage. Hasty investigation in order to achieve quick results may lead to an undeserved acquittal.

5

Records of Finding on Alternative Charges by the Court Martial

"There is no worse torture than the torture of laws."

Bacon

In certain situations the officer framing the charge is doubtful whether the offence so capable of being proved by legal evidence is more accurately described by one word or expression, or by another. In such cases he may frame two or more alternative charges, each charge containing one of the words or expressions which appear to the officer to be applicable to the facts as capable of proof.

In the disposal of the disciplinary cases in the Army the recourse to framing of alternative charges was meant to be taken in doubtful cases. While giving an illustration it had been pointed out on page 105 in *The Constitution and Practice of Courts Martial* by Thomas Frederick Simmons and published by John Murray, London 1873, edition that, "In cases where a soldier is found in possession of or dealing with property not his own, and can give no satisfactory account of it, and it is uncertain he was the actual thief or not, it is irregular to frame a single charge in the disjunctive. This had been previously held at the Judge Advocate General office, but was very distinctly pointed out by the JAG in 1867, and the new regulations supply a form of two charges in the alternative, (1) the one for stealing, the other for receiving the property knowing it to be stolen. Mowbray pointed out that the court may, "then find the prisoner guilty of either charge and acquit him of the other, or may acquit him of both charges according to the preponderance of the evidence".

Another example was given on page 33 of *The Hand Book of Military Law* by Capt R J Wilkins and W S Chaney, 1930 edition, with the explanation "It is wrong to frame more than one charge in respect of one and the same set of facts unless the additional charges are alternative: for example, a soldier breaks out of barracks in order to visit a place which is out.of bounds; it is not wrong to charge him (1) breaking out of barracks, (2) being found in a place prohibited by garrison orders".

Illustration

Rules of Procedure as contained in *The Manual of Military Law*, published for the British Army state in Rule 15, "offences may be charged in the alternative in separate charges but in no case shall they be charged in the alternative in the same charge. When charges are laid in the alternative they should be set out in order of gravity, commencing with the most serious.

To illustrate, a person may be charged with reckless driving in one charge and alternatively with careless driving in another charge". Similar provisions exist in the Army Rules framed for the Indian Army. It is to cater to above situations that alternative charges are framed against the accused persons at their trials by court martial convened under the

Army Act. These charges are all inserted and form part of one charge sheet prepared for the trial of the accused. Note to Army Rule 28 stipulates that all charges including the alternative charges, must be consecutively numbered. As a matter of practice the most serious of two or more alternative charges are placed first in the charge sheet.

An endeavour has been made in this paper to analyse the provisions pertaining to the procedure to be adopted by the courts with regard to record of their findings and the requirements of noting down the brief reasons by way of "Speaking Order" in such cases.

When there is one charge laid in the alternative, then the charge sheet will obviously contain minimum two charges. Army Rules lay down certain procedural provisions to regulate the conduct of trial in such contingencies. Where an accused person pleads guilty to the first of two or more charges laid in the alternative, the prosecutor may, after the court has explained to the accused the implication of his plea of guilty, and before the accused is arraigned on the alternative charge or charges, withdraw such alternative charge or charges without requiring the accused to plead thereto. The aim here is to avoid unnecessary and prolonged hardship when the ends of justice can be said to have met by the accused offering a plea of guilty on one charge. Of course a record to that effect is required to be made upon the proceedings of the court. However, if such a course has been adopted, the accused will not be entitled to a verdict on the alternative charges. The reason being that he would not have been arraigned upon them and the court would not have the benefit of hearing evidence with regard to the same so as to decide if he is guilty of the charge.

How should a trial proceed in such cases ? Army Rule 54 relating to procedure after plea of guilty provides that if there are alternative charges, the court may either proceed with respect to all the charges as if the accused had not pleaded guilty to any charge. Otherwise instead of trying him, the court may record a finding of "guilty" upon any of the alternative charges to which he has pleaded guilty and a finding of "not guilty" upon all the other alternative charges.

It also stands to logic that when there is an alternative charge, then one of the two charges will be more serious in nature. The Rules stipulate that where alternative charges are preferred and the accused pleads "Not Guilty" to the charge which alleges the more serious offence and "Guilty" to the other, the court shall try him as if he had pleaded "Not Guilty" to all the charges.

Army Rule 62

How is the finding to be recorded and how shall the reasons be spelt out in the court martial proceedings ? In the original text of the Army Act as enacted in 1950 there was no requirement to give a speaking order. It was held in R Shanmugain's case that the nature of proceedings before a court martial are summary in nature and hence, there is no need for a detailed judgement or even discussion of evidence. The decision of the court as recorded in R Shanmughain V OC 65 Coy ASC, 1984 (1) SLR 109 refers. However, the Rules have since undergone amendment.

The relevant law with regard to speaking order is contained in clauses (1) and (7) of Army Rule 62 which read as under:

1. The findings on every charge upon which the accused is arraigned shall be recorded as finding of "Guilty" or of "Not Guilty". After recording the finding of each charge, the court shall give brief reasons in support thereof. The judge advocate or, if there is none, the presiding officer, shall record or cause to be recorded

such brief reasons in the proceedings. The above record shall be signed and dated by the presiding officer and the judge advocate, if any.

2. The court shall not find the accused guilty on more than one of two or more charges laid down in the alternative, even if conviction upon the charge necessarily connotes guilt upon the alternative charge or charges."

The procedure is quite simple when the accused pleads "guilty" to the first charge contained in a charge sheet having other alternative charges and such alternative charges are withdrawn. But there may be situations when either the accused pleads "Not Guilty" to all such charges or "Not Guilty" to the serious but "Guilty" to remaining ones. Visualise a contingency where three charges have been framed against the accused out of which the second and third charges are alternative charges. The trial has proceeded on plea of "not guilty" put forth for each of the charges. If while deliberating on their findings, the court finds the accused guilty of the first charge, then going by a plain reading of Clause 7 of Army Rule 62, no deliberation needs to be done upon the evidence with regard to second and third charges. Such a view may be taken in the light of the provision which states that "the court shall not find the accused guilty on more than one of two or more charges laid down in the alternative".

In such a scenario after the court had found the accused guilty of the first charge, it should cease to analyse evidence any further while deliberating on the findings and proceed to record a finding of "not guilty" with regard to second and third charges in a mechanical fashion. However, it may be pointed out that there is a legal requirement for the court to give brief reasons in support of its findings on each charge by virtue of amended provisions of Army Rule 62(1). In this case, suppose the court did not peruse the evidence on second and third charges. Accordingly, the court would find itself unable to give reasons (speaking order) except with regard to the first charge. Hence, it would omit to give brief reasons with regard to second and third charges.

Legally Desirable

But would this be the legally desirable procedure to adopt? In my opinion it would not be prudent to adhere to the procedure outlined above. In this regard we should be guided by the provisions of Clause 1 and 7 of Army Rule 62. A careful reading of these provisions lead us to certain clear conclusions.

Firstly, the court is required to record their findings with regard to each charge contained in the charge sheet. It is immaterial whether the charges are alternative or not. Findings with respect to each charge is required to be recorded. Trial will remain incomplete if the findings have not been recorded on each charge contained in the charge sheet. Secondly, such record of findings can only be made by the court after it has deliberated on the evidence with regard to each charge. There is no way in which a court may record its findings on a charge on which plea of "not guilty" has been advanced without considering the evidence. Hence, it logically follows that unless the court examines the evidence with regard to any charge and then proceeds to record its findings with regard to the same charge, the provisions of Army Rule 62(1) would stand contravened. Fourthly, there may be situations with regard to alternative charges where conviction upon one charge necessarily connotes guilt upon the alternative charges. In that scenario, the court has to deliberate and decide as to with regard to which charge it would be more appropriate for the accused to be found "guilty".

Therefore, the evidence with regard to various charges has to be very critically examined to decide as to its suitability in reference to conviction on the charge. For example, the evidence may disclose that the findings of "guilty" is required to be recorded to each of three charges. Yet the evidence may specifically meet the ingredients of one particular charge say third charge more than the other two charges laid in the alternative. In that case, the court is expected to record a finding of "guilty" on third and "not guilty" on the first and second charges.

It would, therefore, be legally desirable that while deliberating on their findings the courts martial must examine and consider their findings with regard to each charge even when there are two or more charges in the alternative. Moreover, the courts martial must also record brief reasons with reference to each charge contained in the charge sheet.

6

In House Remedies Against Court Martial Verdicts

> "Machinery for securing justice is equally, if not more, important than rights."
>
> Justice G S Pathak

The Army Act, 1950 (Act XLVI of 1950) is a self contained Act, it is a special law designed to cater for the special dictates of the military discipline and the service conditions of the Army personnel.

Trial by courts martial is one of the effective modes provided under the Army Act for the administration of justice within the Army. The Act contains well defined provisions to provide an effective remedy to persons aggrieved by the orders of courts martial. Such a relief may be claimed at any stage in the course of a disciplinary process irrespective of the fact whether or not the findings and sentence of a court martial have been confirmed or in relation to a trial by Summary Courts Martial where such confirmation is not required. Such an alternative is also ipso-facto available to the superior authorities under a separate provision laid out in the Army Act. The relevant law in this regard is contained in Army Act, Sections 164 and 179 respectively. These remedies are open not only to the persons tried and convicted by courts martial but in certain cases to the higher commanders when they wish to grant pardon or remission to the persons tried and convicted by a court martial.

In the case of Mulkh Raj V UOI; 1983 Cri LJ 1794 (J&K), it was held that, "Making a representation to the confirming authority by an accused against the conviction recorded by a court martial, seeking a review of his conviction after its confirmation by the competent authority in terms of sub sections (1) and (2) of Section 164 relates to his personal liberty".

There does appear at times some ambiguity in understanding the scope and application of the ibid two sections. An attempt has been made in this article to study the salient differences in the intent and purpose of the above sections.

Clause (2) of Section 164 provides that, "Any person subject to this Act who considers himself aggrieved by a finding or sentence of any court martial which has been confirmed may present a petition to the Central Government, the Chief of Army Staff or any prescribed officer superior in command to the one who confirmed such finding or sentence and the Central Government, the Chief of the Army Staff or the other officer as the case may be, may pass such order thereon as it or he thinks fit". Various prescribed officers in context of this Section have been enumerated in Army Rule 201.

The provisions relating to a right to prefer post confirmation petition have been designed somewhat with the identical aim which is underlying for the civilians and contained in Sections 372 to 394 of Cr PC, 1974 relating to appeals against the judgement or order of criminal court. However, it needs to Sec 164 is not a right to prefer an appeal. That is so because no right to appeal as such is contemplated under the scheme of the Army Act. What it lays down is the remedy to submit a petition. The Supreme Court had clearly held that the right to prefer an appeal is a right created by statute. In M Ramnarain (P) Ltd V STC; AIR 1983 SC 786, it remarked that, "No party can file an appeal against any judgement, decree or order as a matter of course in the absence of a suitable provision of some law conferring on the party concerned the right to file an appeal against any judgement, decree or order".

Section 164

The provisions of Section 164 (2) make it apparent that firstly, the remedy under the above clause is available to any person aggrieved by any finding or sentence of a court martial. Secondly, such a remedy is not attracted till such time the courts martial is concluded. Therefore, during the pendency of a court martial, the role of this Section does not come into play. Thirdly, the person aggrieved may well be the accused or any other person. Thus, for example, a witness, prosecutor or the defending officer of a court martial can also move a petition seeking remedies under this clause with regard to their grievances, if they have any.

Such a person as is discussed here has to be necessarily subject to the Act. The section does not by implication altogether debar a retired person to avail of this right. As long as such retired person was subject to the Act when he felt aggrieved, or when the cause of action arose, he can move for an operation of this clause. A person who may have been tried and convicted by a court martial and having been dismissed or cashiered from service and where the finding or the sentence have since been confirmed can claim a remedy under this clause although he would no longer be subject to the Act. He would acquire such a right in view of coming into play the provisions of Section 123 (3) which state "When a person subject to this Act is sentenced by a court martial to imprisonment for life or imprisonment, this Act shall apply to him during the terms of his sentence, though he is cashiered or dismissed from the regular Army, or has otherwise ceased to be subject to this Act and he may be kept, removed, imprisoned and punished as if he continued to be subject to this Act".

It is thus obvious that the provisions of Section 123 (3) where applicable, do not merely relate to keeping, removal, imprisonment and punishment. It would be unfair and unequitious to hold that after ceasing to be subject to the Act, though such a person can be kept, removed, imprisoned or punished but cannot be allowed the right to seek a remedy being aggrieved by the court martial

Similarly, benefit under Clause (2) of Section 164 is also to be extended to a person who has since ceased to be of subject to the Army Act, for example, or reaching the age of superannuation and wishes to present a post confirmation petition seeking remedy against a court martial verdict relating to the period when he was in Army service. In light of the aforesaid, the benefit of ibid Clause (2) may in such cases, be claimed by persons who are no more subject to the Act. Since the above clause is being used in a manner advantageous to the accused persons and cannot in any way be labelled as prejudicial to their interest, apparently no view to the contrary has been taken so far by the judiciary. Notwithstanding the same, this clause needs to be suitably reworded so as to remove the ambiguity as regards its applicability.

No Limitation Period

The clause, while conferring a right to present a post confirmation petition on a person who considers himself aggrieved by a finding or sentence of any court martial which has been confirmed casts a corresponding duty on the competent authority to consider such petition but does not prescribe any period of limitation. No limitation has been fixed in law for filing a post confirmation petition. It was held that the relevant statute imposes no time limit for the exercise of such right and the performance of such duty as ruled by the High Court in the case of J C Sharma Vs UOI, 1985 Cri LJ 696 (Himachal). Further it was ruled that the removal from service under Army Rule 19 is not a bar for the appropriate authorities to entertain the post confirmation petition subsequently. Competent authority must determine whether there is evidence to sustain conviction and sentence of the petitioner. In the above case, the removal of the petitioner from service was set aside. Further, the respondents were directed to consider the representation of the petitioner as a post confirmation petition under Section 164 (2) and dispose it on merit. In this manner , the scope of section 164 (2) was considerably enlarged.

The Section does not provide that the decision on a post confirmation petition should be in the form of.a speaking order. It also does not give a right to be personally heard. In the case of Sidhu KNS, Lt Col V UOI, 1977 (2) SLR 479 Punjab & Haryana, it was held that it was not incumbent on the authority to afford an opportunity for personal hearing before deciding a petition under Section 164 (2) even when the same was asked for by the representationist. Nevertheless, a view is held in certain quarters that a decision to the contrary would have been a more pôsitive and progressive step in line with the cannons of natural justice.

When there was a delay of over eleven years in intimating the decision on a post confirmation petition, the Supreme Court held in the case of Capt Harish Uppal V UOI, SLP Nò 5087 of 1984 that, "It is a well settled policy of law that the parties should pursue their rights and remedies promptly and not sleep over their rights. That is the whole policy behind the limitation Act and other rule of limitation". In another case which related to Maj G S Sodhi V UOI; WP (Cri) No 478 of 1989 the Supreme Court observed that, "a post confirmation petition cannot vitiate the verdict passed by the court martial and the confirmation thereon, even if this petition is not disposed off".

While deciding a petition under Section 164 the authority is not required to issue a speaking order. Thus the affected person is denied the satisfaction about application of mind having taken place in his matter. This controversy was finally set at rest by the Supreme Court in the case of S N Mukherjee V UOI; 1990 Cri LJ 2148 (SC) when it observed that "Reasons are not required to be recorded for an order passed by the confirming authority confirming the finding and sentence recorded by court martial as well as for the order passed by the Central Government dismissing the past confirmation petition".

Section 179

The other section which can be used to provide relief against the sentence of a court martial is contained in Section 179 of the Army Act. The ibid section provides that, "When any person subject to this Act has been convicted by a court martial of an offence, the Central Government or the Chief of the Army Staff, or, in the case of a sentence, which he could have confirmed or which did not require confirmation, the officer commanding the Army, Army Corps, Division or Independent Brigade in which such person at the time of conviction was serving or the prescribed officer may:

(a) Either with or without conditions, which the person sentenced accepts, pardon the person or remit the whole or any part of the punishment awarded; or

(b) mitigate the punishment awarded; or

The accused has prepared his Defence Sir !

SINCE YOU WERE 'ABSENT WITHOUT LEAVE, YOU WILL BE GIVEN 'DISMISSAL' FROM THE SERVICE
SAAB! IT WILL BE GIVEN FROM THE QM STORE OR I WILL GET IT FROM THE CSD.
YASEEN

(c) commute such punishment for any less punishment or punishments mentioned in this Act;

(d) either with or without conditions which the person sentenced accepts release the person on parole.

The above Section has to be read together with the Army Rule 204. Analysis of the above Section discloses that these provisions are attracted firstly in respect of any person subject to the Act and secondly with regard to one who has been convicted. This is also applicable in the case of one who was at some point of time subject to the Act but after his conviction by a court martial has ceased to be subject to the Act. Thirdly, to bring the case within the purview of this Section, the person ought to have been convicted by a court martial of any offence. Having regard to a General Court Martial, District Court Martial or Summary General Court Martial this Section will only come into operation when the proceedings have been confirmed.

Fourthly, the laid down powers can be exercised by the prescribed authorities on their own. While no petition by the aggrieved person is required, yet the person concerned may certainly propel the authorities by presenting a petition praying for invoking the powers available to them under Section 179. The authorities may decide that the relief intended to be provided will only become applicable if the conditions as decided by them are acceptable to the offender. The provisions of Section 179 are analogus to the powers similarly conferred upon Sections 432 to 435 of the Cr PC, 1974 for suspension, remission and commutation of sentences.

Comparison of Two Sections

A comparison of the provisions contained in Sections 164(2) and 179 shows marked differences as regards the scope, object, application and powers available under each. While the former affords a remedy to an aggrieved person which he can pray for as a matter of right, the latter gives powers to the competent authorities. Consideration of his case under Section 179 cannot be demanded as a matter of right by an accused. To obtain relief under Section 164(2), a petition has necessarily to be preferred so as to set in motion the operation of the Section. In the case of Section 179, the authorities can suo motu proceed to act on their own. The powers to award a remedy under Section 164 are quite wide in view of the words used viz "may pass such order thereon as it or he thinks fit". To illustrate, under Section 164(2) orders may be passed restoring acting rank or in some other case directing payment of back wages to a person who submits a petition. On the other hand, the powers available under Section 179 have been specifically enumerated under Clause (a) to (d) and are thus in scope clearly limited. They cannot be used for purposes other than ordering pardon, remission, mitigation, commutation or release of the person on parole.

Further, in Section 164 (2), the powers are only available to the officers superior to the confirming authority. After having once confirmed the proceedings, the confirming authority ceases to hold any power over the finding or sentence, except to append his recommendations in the channel. On the other hand, under Section 179 the confirming authority has also been invested with the jurisdiction to exercise the powers of pardon and remission.

While Section 164 (2) can be put to use when submitting an application against any finding or sentence inflicted by a Court Martial; Section 179 only governs those cases where some punishment has been awarded by a Court Martial. In other words, while relief can be claimed under Section 164(2) both against finding or sentence of a court martial; the finding is immune from the scope of relief under Section 179 except that a pardon granted under Section 179(a) would take away the conviction and thereby as an indirect consequence the finding would also vanish.

In the case of a petition under Section 164 (2), no time limit has been laid down prescribing the period within which a remedy is to be sought. Therefore, at any time after the conclusion of a trial, the aggrieved person may submit a petition praying for remedy. On the other hand, once the convict has been set free after completion of the terms of imprisonment awarded to him by a court martial the operation of Section 179 would become meaningless. This is because at that stage remission, commutation or mitigation would all become infructuous for him and so would be his release on parole.

Independent Scope

The Act nowhere mentions that scope of Army Act Section 179 is to be seen in context of Section 164. The statute does not state that while dealing with a petition under Army Act Section 164, the power of the authorities are limited to the reliefs listed in Section 179. In fact the two sections are quite independent of each other. Hence, there can be little doubt that even when remedies under Section 164A have been exhausted, the role of Section 179 does not get extinguished.

The Army Act also contains provisions for suspension of sentence of life imprisonment or imprisonment. As laid down in Section 182, irrespective of the fact whether or not an offender has already been committed to prison or to military custody, the Central Government, the Chief of the Army Staff or officers empowered to convene a General or District Court Martial may suspend such a sentence. Such a provision was devised so that during military exigencies, situations may emerge where even convicts have to be used for essential duties of military nature. The power of suspension of sentence places in the hands of a commander a means of clemency and within reach of an offender an opportunity to redeem his character. The statute does not provide any right to a person to demand suspension of his sentence as a matter of right. Notwithstanding the same, since such a provision stands incorporated in the statute and it would be of substantial help to him, the accused can certainly move a petition praying that such provisions may be invoked in his case.

In view of the aforesaid, a proper understanding of the scope and ambit of the provisions of the above two sections can be effectively made use of against the verdicts of courts martial. Persons affected may take recourse to these remedies before deciding to adopt the alternative of litigation in the civil court.

7

Futuristic Trends in Military Laws

> Our judicial system is too exotic, too expansive, too protracted, too elitist and too pyramidal for the weaker section to seek and secure justice.
>
> Justice V R Krishna Iyer.

In the course of the last decade and half, more changes were introduced to the system of Military Justice than in the preceding half century. After its enactment in 1950 for the first time major amendments were brought to the Army Act during 1993. Some of these changes were quite sustantial in nature. One of the changes proceeded to give an altogether new meaning to the period of limitation for trial and thereby to subjection to the Army Act of an offender who has gone out or superannuated from service. That was brought about by way of changes introduced to the text of Sections 122 and 123 of the Army Act. Field punishment was entirely deleted from the statute. An accused person came to be furnished with a copy of the court martial proceedings soon after the conclusion of his trial so that he could meaningfully exercise his right of seeking a pre-confirmation review of the proceedings.

Legal system as existing in the Army also underwent some major improvements. An Institute of Military Law (IML) was set up at Kamptee near Nagpur to impart training in Military Law. Women officers were inducted to serve in the Judge Advocate General's (JAG) Department. Legal Cells were set up at the seats of nine High Courts and the Supreme Court of India to effectively defend the cases relating to defence personnel in such courts. The age old Manual of Indian Military Law was replaced by the bi-lingual manual of Military Law. A comprehensive review of the Regulations for the Army was carried out and a revised edition published. A corps day was specified for the JAG's Department and (without being a regiment) the department came to have its first Colonel of the Regiment.

In the aftermath of the above sweeping changes and reforms it would be interesting to comprehend and visualise the size, shape and role of the JAG's Deptt in next two or three decades. What are the changes anticipated and considered desirable in the system of judicial administration? Without drawing strength from the ongoing official thinking, this article aims to attempt to put forth a conceptual hypothesis in this regard.

While the demand for setting up a National Security Council is gathering momentum for better management of defence matters at macro level, we need to introduce a common Military Code for the three Services. This could be structured on the pattern of Unified Court of Military Justice set up for the US Army. Such a common code would bring about uniformity in the conditions of service, privileges as also the liabilities of the military personnel belonging to the three services. It would facilitate framing of statutory rules on service conditions of the combatants. The mode of trial by courts martial and the procedure for dispensation of justice will be identical for all military personnel rather than differ with the colour of uniform worn by them.

Services Tribunal

The proposal to establish an Armed Forces Courts Martial and Administrative Tribunal is already under active consideration of the Government. The Tribunal will be competent to hear matters when the vires of statutory provisions are questioned. It will also have the power to test the vires of subordinate legislations and rules. The proposed forum will afford a meaningful opportunity to the accused persons of being actually heard in person or being represented through their counsel at the appeallate stage in the matters relating to courts martial awárds or conditions of service. Not all service personnel, even though deserving, can be automatically promoted to the higher ranks in the Armed Forces where the rank structure is like a pyramid. Aggrieved with the result of the promotion boards or other decisions like fixation of pay, seniority, grant of accommodation, confirmation or confidential reports etc., these military men presently exercise the right of first seeking an appeallate remedy through statutory complaints and then move for writ petitions, calling for intervention and judicial review. The proposed Tribunal would seek to reduce the delay in disposal of such cases by prompt adjudication. While deciding the composition of such a Tribunal, the recommendations of the Malimath Committee report and the observations of the Supreme Court in the case of L. Chandra Kumar Civil Appeal No. 481 of 1989 need to be borne in mind. Such a forum will be invested with the requisite jurisdiction to decide the cases put forth by the personnel belonging to all the three services. While performing the role of a first appeallate Court, all decisions of the Tribunal, whether created pursuant to Artile 323 A or Article 323 B of the Constitution, will be subject to the High Court writ jurisdiction under Articles 226/227 before a Division Bench of the High Court within whose territorial jurisidiction the particular Bench would fall.

The need to spell out reasons in matters involving rights or liabilities of people has been unambiguously highlighted by the Supreme Court. While deciding Siemens Engineering & Manufacturing Co V UOI, AIR 1976 SC 1785, their Lordships had held that, "It is now well settled that where an authority makes an order in exercise of a quasi-judicial function, it must record its reasons in support of the order it makes. Every quasi-judicial order must be supported by reasons. The rule requiring reasons to be given in support of an order, is like the principle of audi-alteram partem, a basic principle of natural justice which must inform every quasi-judicial process and this rule must be observed in its proper spirit and mere pretence of compliance with it would not satisfy the requirement of law".

Already changes have been introduced to the Army Act whereby brief reasons are required to be recorded by Courts Martial in support of their findings. This is applicable to all courts martial except summary courts martial. It is desirable that even summary courts martial should be called upon to give speaking orders. This should be obligatory in cases where accused persons offer a plea of "not guilty". Such a measure will reduce chances of misuse of the procedures and also usher in perceptible evidence of application of mind by the officers holding the trial. Need for justification for such a suggestion springs forth from the vast powers entrusted to a commanding officer whereby he can curtail liberty of an accused by award of rigorous imprisonment upto one year and also deprive him of his means of livelihood.

The provisions with regard to the execution of sentences meted out to service personnel by courts martial deserve a relook so as to make them more liberal. Unnecessary hardship caused to their family members and relatives should be removed. In a given case, a military convict undergoing life imprisonment and belonging to Punjab was lodged at Civil Prison, Dibrugarh (Assam). His wife filed a writ petition praying that he be shifted from Assam to Patiala. In this case of Balwinder Kaur V. UOI; Punjab & Haryana High Court CWP No 9759 of 1993, the court ordered that to avoid any dehumanising effect on the prisoner, he should be kept at a place where he can have access to his near and dear ones.

In the coming years the Services may decide to organise the Judge Advocate General Department on an integrated basis for the three wings of the defence forces. This would be in keeping with the pattern of the professionals belonging to the Army Medical Corps, the Army Dental Corps or the Military Nursing Service. The officers would be liable to be transferred from the Army to the Navy or Air Force and also the other way around. The main advantage will be in the form of integration of legal manpower and other resources besides consequential saving in manpower with regard to the apparatus provided for defence of court cases. This would continue to be relevant even after setting up of the Tri-service tribunal for the simple reason that the jurisdiction of the High Courts would continue to exist particularly in matters seeking judicial review. With regard to the organisation of the Department itself; it may be bifurcated into pre-trial and post trial wings. The pre-trial functions may be fully insulated by way of entrusting these to a Directorate of Litigation which should be set up. The officers of the JAG's Department would come to be invested with the right of audience to represent the Union before various courts and tribunals.

Judicial Service

The service rendered by the officers of the Judge Advocate General's Department being reckonable as Judicial Service, would enable utilising the professional expertise and experience of such officers in all related fields. They may be designated as judges empowered to hold TADA courts and nominated to assist other tribunals, higher judiciary and other deputational assignments.

The officers of the JAG Department would come to play a dominating role to assist the commanders decide cases objectively on the merits. It would become legally imperative to base decisions purely on objective considerations. The Madhya Pradesh High Court had held in Lt Col Sunil Bawa's case (1994(8) SLR 253) that the Central Government is under the constitutional obligation to consider the petitioner's grievances objectively and dispose off the same by a reasoned order. Reasoned decision is not only for the purpose of showing that the citizen is receiving justice but is also a valid discipline in any quasi-judicial order. Executive actions and the orders of the commanders would henceforth be subjected to more critical judicial and legal scrutiny. That would necessitate that the services of the officers with legal background will come to be greatly needed for posting to different organisations like Military Engineering Services (MES), Border Roads Organisation, Army Schools run by Army Welfare Education Society, Ordnance Factories, Canteen Stores Department (CSD), Assam Rifles, Rashtriya Rifles, National Cadet Corps, National Security Guard (NSG), Army Group Insurance and Army Welfare Housing Organisation (AWHO) etc.

Coming years will devote in a big way to address the issues relating not only to the men but also to members belonging to the fair sex. Substantive laws giving woman equality and clothing her with rights is important because it is currently deficient. The Army has thrown open its doors to women and it is no more an exclusive preserve of men. The status of the officers belonging to the Military Nursing Service deserve to be clearly defined. Consequent upon induction of women in the Army, rules and regulations need to be reshaped to cater for maintenance of discipline among them. Suitable provisions would be required to be inserted in the Military Law for the detention, investigation of charges and punishments awardable to the members of the weaker sex.

Rajasthan High Court in the case of Mt Choki V The State; AIR 1957 RAJ 11 had conceded that it was open to a court to grant bail to a woman even in cases where she was accused of an offence which was punishable with death or transportation for life. The ruling given supra sets the tone in so far as approach of the higher judiciary is concerned in dealing with cases involving women offenders. The Supreme Court had in the case of Nargesh Mirza V IAC; 1981 (2) SLJ 349 (SC) opined that Articles 15 (I) and 16 (2) of the Constitution do not prohibit the State from making discrimination on the ground of sex coupled with other considerations.

It is expected that the coming decades would see provision being made for legal cover at the grass root level. It is visualised that at least one officer from the JAG's Department will be available at each station and brigade level to render legal advice. Presently even simple matters like courts of inquiry, summary of evidence and summary courts martial proceedings have to be referred to Corps or Command level for advice and opinion simply because an officer from JAG's Department is not available at lower formations. Such a step would result in making available one officer with the legal qualifications per almost 6000 troops. The accused persons under trial and those at the pre-trial stage deserve to be provided a statutory right to seek intervention of the JAG where they find inordinate delays or deprivation of basic legal rights to them. The augmentation of JAG set up will provide them a meaningful opportunity to approach for an early and sympathetic deal.

Computerisation

The vast quantum of reference material available in the form of Army Orders, instructions and policy letters all deserve to be converted into a well classified and comprehensive data bank so that the collection, collation and interpretation of the information will be simplified. Similarly the case law pertaining to various courts including tribunals can be easily made accessible if it is stored in computers. Through an integrated system network these should be available down to corps and division level. The case law based on the decisions arrived at by the courts martial should also be compiled on the lines of the rulings given by the tribunals of income tax, sales tax and custom and central excise etc. The decisions given by courts martial can then be cited as precedent where the facts appear to be similar.

There would be a sea change in the field of education in Military Law. Suggestions from the formations may induce reversion to the earlier practice of Military Law being made a compulsory paper for the Staff College entrance exam. Junior leaders including JCOs will be detailed to attend basic courses in Military Law at the Institute of Military Law. Short capsules in Military Law would be made obligatory for officers selected to hold "A" staff appointments. In addition syllabus at the Corps of Military Police Training School and Intelligence Corps School will come to acquire the desired course contents based on law. The officers from other two services and para military forces would also attend courses of instruction conducted at the IML. Research and analytical studies will be undertaken by the faculty specially set up for the purpose at the IML so as to carry out diagonostic survey of disciplinary cases. IML will also be designated as the nodal agency for imparting teaching in the International Humanitarian Law within the defence forces.

An insight into the role played by the JAG's Department of the US Army during the famous "Desert Shield" operations will provide a valuable clue as to likely utililty of the department during war conditions. As part of legal support for deploying soldiers, Judge Advocates at more than 60 army installations attended briefing for more than 2,00,000 soldiers. During such briefings, the Judge Advocates explained the nature and legal effect of general and special powers of attorney. They spoke about circumstances under which making of wills were appropriate. The effect of commercial life insurance policies containing exclusionary war clauses was highlighted by them. After the interview of the soldier clients they were given individually tailored legal documents. Judge Advocates prepared more than 40,000 wills and 70,000 powers of attorney. This herculean task was accomplished through the Legal Automation Army Wide System (LAAWS).

Family Support Counselling

Judge Advocates of the US Army also held family support briefings back home in military cantonments. At these sessions, critical information was provided to the families of the soldiers as to what was really happening in the Iraq War. It was noted that at these community centres, families sought legal assistance in greater numbers than when soldiers were in garrison.

In the identical manners it is expected that the officers of the JAG's Department in India may be required in the days ahead to provide counselling and hold family courts for the soldiers and families. Women officers serving in the JAG's Department will be specially employed for such purposes. These facilities are specially needed for the troops in smaller cantonments such as Pulgaon, Namkum, Nasirabad, Binaguri, Lalgarh etc., where the civil expertise in this field is not suitably available.

Other innovative trends may involve the jurisdiction of Lok Adalats being expanded to the motor accident cases or where compensation is to be paid to victims of firing range accidents. On one hand, it will cut-short delays in disposal of such cases and on the other reduce the financial burden by way of payment of interest and litigation expenses which are to be invariably undergone by the Government.

Greater thought will come to be given to the selection of members to serve on courts martial. It needs to be decided at the appropriate level whether the members should be given some training in the rudiments of judicial procedure, judicial objectivity, judicial reasoning and the like. Should they be made to go through orientation courses and get some idea of the laws; substantive and procedural, prior to their assumption of duties at the courts martial ? Such a concept has emerged from the decision of the Supreme Court when, sounding a note of caution in the case of Major G S Sodhi, AIR 1981 SC 1617; it held that, "It is to be borne in mind that the authorities are entrusted with certain powers and duties under the Act which also enjoined on them certain important reponsibilities particularly in the matter of holding the enquiries and trials. The Parliament in its wisdom in exercise of its powers under Article 33 has enacted the Army Act and the officers are to be guided by factors like exigencies of service, maintenance of discipline in the Army, speedier trial, the nature of the offence and person against whom the offence is committed. Normally having regard to the high office they hold, there should not be any scope to apprehend deliberate lapse or intentional on their part".

The charter of duties of the officers of the JAG's Department will be enlarged so as to render legal opinion on matters like taxation, cantonment laws, rent control and eviction cases, laws relating to marriage and divorce, maintenance, dowry, wills, environment, ecology and wild life preservation etc.

In case the changes thus propounded appear to be quite fantastic then the words of VI Lenin need to be remembered,"Without a revolutionary theory there can be no revolutionary movement".

8

Management of Indian Legal System and Reforms in Judiciary

"If the law be dishonestly administered, the salt has not its flavour. If be weakly or fitfully enforced, the guarantees of order fail, for it is more by the certainity than by the severity of punishment that offenders are repressed. If the lamp of justice goes in darkness, how great is the darkness."

Viscount Bryce

The higher judiciary in our country has acquited itself with glory in the recent years. Despite its many imperfections, the rule of law is one of the best things going for India. Major scandals like Hawala, Urea, Housing scam and Chandraswamy episode would have remained burried under executive wraps but for the interest shown by the judiciary. When the bureaucracy and the elected representatives were both found wanting, the Courts rose up to the expectations by asking for a probe in these areas. The Apex Court moved to properly rein in Mr. T N Seshan when it found that certain actions of the then Chief Election Commissioner deserved to be censured.

Notwithstanding the same, it is an open secret that a lot more needs to be done for the legal system as is existing in the country. Justice M Hidayatullah had once remarked that, "the cost of litigation and the law's delays tend to frustrate the common man in his quest for justice in this behalf. The common man is entitled to have his case heard and decided impartially and with expedition. Justice delayed is (justice) denied. But in this connection the common man is hit hard by the multiplicity of hastily enacted laws some of which are badly drafted, the enormous fees demanded by lawyers and the court fees that have to be paid. Added to this there is a cumbersome procedure which the court must follow and of which one side or the other is ever ready to take full advantage of. The numerous appeals and revisions to which the decisions of courts and tribunals are successively subject are further impediments to speedy justice". The total number of cases pending in the various High Courts and the lower Courts add upto more than 25 million. The Apex Court has succeeded in reducing pendency in the last few years - especially from mid 1994 - from over 1,34,000 to the current figure of 22,000 (comprising roughly half miscellaneous admission matters and half final regular hearing cases). The subject of arrears reduction has become topical. There have been cases which still remain on the list and are undecided for over a decade. The agony and plight of the under trials is pathetic. In some cases the process of law has been misused and hijacked by unscrupulous use of public interest litigation.

Confidence Inspiring and Alert

Allegations of corruption, favouritism and other misdeeds had been levelled against a number of senior judges and in one case even against a then sitting judge of the Apex Court. In its editorial titled "Not above the law - Judges are as much fallible and human as others", *Indian Express*, Delhi, wrote on 26 March 1997, "There can be no disputing that the judiciary is by and large fair and its performance has been far more confidence inspiring than that of the executive and the legislature. There is no practical way to bring to book a corrupt and adament judge. While the black sheep may be few and far between, the system cannot over look their presence except at a cost to the impartlality and fairness of the judiciary".

An alert and effective judiciary is of paramount importance for proper functioning of the democracy. Conversely, disappearance of faith in the judicial system of the country may lead to social and political anarchy. The judiciary is an autonomous arm of the state; it must not become subservient to the executive. There are social ramifications of making the judiciary a self perpetuating body. In the prevailing national scene the social and political turbulence in different parts of the country can be attributed to a certain extent to the lack of faith in the courts and consequential disillusionment on the part of the people to seek justice from judicial tribunals.

Such a state of the Indian legal system has also contributed to impede the corporate growth of our country to some extent. Frequent changes in the statutory provisions have only added to the misery of the business managers who are usually not well versed in law. On one hand, the plethora of codified laws and subordinate legislation have confused the managers about the letter and spirit of the legal provisions. On the other, it has contributed to the delay in effective and speedy finalisation of cases relating to corporate matters. Moreover, the delay in disposal of the court cases has prompted the business world to devise ways and means to meander their way through administrative lethargy. Taking a cue from their example, it has induced the law abiding section to adopt short cuts to the irksome procedures.

Causes of the Malady

It would not be difficult to diagnose the causes of this malady. The first and foremost reason is the lengthy legal process. It is the procedures and the rules which together with the manner of their implementation contribute to the delay in settlement of disputes. Secondly, the system is not client-friendly. The corporate sector as also the common public is wary of the language used in the legal provisions. It is not practicable for a common man to understand the meaning and intent of the clauses and articles of various Acts. How can he then be expected to adhere to the same. The interpretation of the statutory terms is found to be a difficult task. The answer lies in simplification of legal provisions. A deliberate effort must be made by the Judges to write short judgements.

Another major cause is the wide spread corruption which a section of the public believes to have come to occupy a deep rooted place in the judicial system and more so at the lower level. An honest litigant often finds that his manipulative opponent manages to mould the process to his advantage. Ironically such cases are rarely reported. There is a perpetual fear harboured in the minds of the common people about likelihood of their being held liable for contempt of the court. The same discourages the litigants from formally reporting the cases of corruption. They are not aware of the guiding philosophy spelt out by the Supreme Court in C Ravichandran's case, 1995 SCC (Cri) 953 when it observed that the court must harmonise constitutional values of free criticism and the need for a fearless curial process and its presiding functionary, the judge. The power to punish the contemner granted to the court not because the judges need the protection but because the citizens need an impartial and strong judiciary.

There are a number of senior judges and eminent jurists who are seriously concerned about the malady afflicting our judicial system. Despite their noble intent, more often than not they find themselves unable to do much about it. There could be various reasons for their inability including their failure to secure the necessary public opinion to institute suitable remedial measures. On the other hand, a section of the lawyer fraternity does not wish any changes brought about in the existing system because of their vested interests.

It would be interesting to note that other professionals like the engineers or educationists have come to accept that the administration and management of their profession cannot be left to them alone. Consequently, specialities such as hospital administration or education management etc. have come into existence. It is surprising but true that so far the concepts of management, as existing today, have not been able to make any visible impact on the legal world. Very little is known about any management consultants who have come to acquire expertise in the field of judicial management. Successive law commissions set up by the Union Government have been entrusted with the responsibility of suggesting judicial reforms. It would be pertinent to note that the country has had the benefit of a number of Law Commissions and more than 100 voluminous reports submitted by them. Was any management expert amongst their members? In fact nearly all the members belonged to the legal field. They were not adequately aware about the progress made in the spheres of management of men, money and resources. Similarly, the Law Ministers also were not men well known in the field of management. The only Law Minister of India who was not a lawyer was Dinesh Goswami.

What is to be Done?

What then needs to be done? Regular meetings of the Chief Ministers and the Chief Justice have applied their mind to some of these problems. They have suggested that the principle of checks and balances must be applicable to the judiciary as well. This idea needs to be given a practical shape.

A few other suggestions put forth by them merit immediate implementation. Firstly the concept of time management needs to be introduced in the field of judicial administration. It needs to be tried out as to how to increase the output of the courts including the Supreme Court. Should they be requested to sit beyond working hours? Secondly, there is a definite need to reduce the number of court holidays. Code of ethics need to be drawn which should restrict the judges from being away from their judicial duties for any ceremonial or other functions. Thirdly, specific time schedules need to be laid down for the judges with regard to disposal of cases before them, as also the maximum number of adjournments permissible in a particular case. The heavy work load accepted by the lawyers also at times impedes the speed of disposal of cases. If a ceiling could be laid down to restrict the maximum work that can be undertaken by a chartered accountant or by a company director, why not do the same for lawyers? Another factor which needs to be considered at length is the creation of additional resources. The Goswami proposal to establish a judicial commission to oversee appointment of judges acquires relevance. This proposal of 1990 advocated a collegiate system which could prevent the misuse of judicial appointments for partisan ends. There is a pressing requirement to increase the number of the magistrates and judges. The Constitution may be amended to provide that no vacancy in the higher judiciary shall remain unfilled for more than a month.

Alternative redressal mechanism needs to be strengthened by creation of more tribunals like Lok Adalats, Family Courts and other such forums. Setting up of the Armed Forces Courts Martial and Administrative Tribunal needs to be expedited. Upper ceiling needs to be fixed about the time to be allowed for verbal arguments by the lawyers. The terms of reference being finalised for the future Law Commission should be suitably designed and it should have experts from the field of a management amongst its members. Entrance test for admission to law colleges should be made more objective and strict so that only the deserving students are allowed to take up the study and practice of this profession.

Relief to Victims

To restore and strengthen the faith of litigants in the judicial process, the remedy and relief provided to the victims has got to be real and perceptible. A mere judicial victory or vindication of stand will not suffice to undo the wrong perpetrated in some cases. Cue has to be taken from decision of the Supreme Court in the case of Delhi Domestic Working Women's Forum V UOI; 1995 SCC (Cri) 7 where the Union Government was directed to evolve a scheme for award of compensation to rape victims and their rehabilitation.

A more tolerant view of the constructive and healthy criticism of its working needs to be not only accepted but encouraged by the judiciary. Introduction of information management systems in the processing of court cases and in the maintenance of records is the need of the day. The process of computerisation handled by the experts in the field of information management needs to be dovetailed in the functioning of the courts without further delay. Case tracking devices should be developed to centralise and regularise filing and record keeping as well. This would allow the courts to be easily informed of the procedural position of individual matters, to locate documents and records more promptly, to consolidate matters having identical issues, and to rid the dockets of infructuous matters. Ultimately it should strive for linking of all lower courts in India to a national computerised grid.

To conclude, adoption of the management concepts and information technology need to be undertaken to bring about the desired improvements in the Indian Legal system.

9

Human Rights and the Handling of Disciplinary Cases in the Army

Napoleon Bonaparte had once remarked that, "There are only two forces in the world, the sword and the spirit. In the long run the sword will always be conquered by the spirit". Perhaps these words were one of the motivating remarks that gave rise to the concept of human rights.

The last decade has seen concepts of human rights assuming increasing importance in various spheres relating to the government affairs. These rights protect individuals against the excesses of the State and portray an attempt to save the individual from oppression and injustice. In the overall scenario, such a trend has led to the examination of military law provisions on the human rights scale with a view to fine tune the modern legal thinking.

Article 21 of our Constitution deals with the right to life. This fundamental right is of widest amplitude and it covers a variety of rights. While referring to this right the Supreme Court has held that, "it does not mean mere animal existence or just physical survival. Any form of torture or cruel, inhuman or degrading treatment offensive to human dignity is unconstitutional". The relevance of human rights in the Military Law provisions may be scrutinised under three distinct heads which relate to the processing of disciplinary cases in the Army. These stages pertain to arrest of an offender, his entitlement to legal aid facilities during the process of investigation and lastly his trial by court martial.

It ought to be ensured that a person charged under the Army Act should not be unnecessarily deprived of his freedom when he is accused of an offence triable by the court martial. The Supreme Court had held in the case of Sepoy Bhuwaneshwar Singh V UOI; 1993 (Cri) LJ 3454 (SC) that the protection granted to persons subject to the Act by provisions of Army Act Secs 101 to 103 read with Army Rule 27 would become meaningless if one who is supposed to be the protector of the person concerned acts callously and appears unconcerned with the rights available to such a person. Therefore, the need for the authorities to show concern and also to avoid any callous attitude towards them becomes manifest.

The existing Rules stipulate that it is not obligatory to place a person under arrest when he is accused of having committed an offence under the Army Act. According to Section 101 of the Army Act, any person subject to the Act who is charged with an offence may be taken into military custody. If the offence is not serious it may be investigated and disposed of without placing the offender under arrest. However, in actual practice offenders are generally taken in custody and confined to the unit quarter guards as soon as their lapse comes to surface. An offender may be arrested by any superior officer and also by a junior officer under certain conditions as specified in the said Section. Under certain situations such arrest may also be ordered by a police officer or a magistrate or by the civil authorities or a police officer upon receiving report of desertion. Arrest could also be carried out by the provost marshall of the Corps of military police or on the orders of a court martial.

In the case of Girija Barua Smt V UOI; 1993 (1) Gauhati Law Journal 169, the Supreme Court had laid bare its views regarding the authority vested in the army authorities to place an offender into arrest thus, "Where there is a reasonable suspicion that a person may commit cognizable offence it may be absolutely necessary to arrest him in order to prevent him from committing the crime. This is a power vested in ordinary civil police under the Cr PC. This power has been conferred on specified Army authorities by virtue of the (Army) Act. We don't think, merely because the repository of the power is different from the civil police authority the court should alter its approach to the question of interfering with contemplated arrest which is a step-in-aid of investigation or of prevention of cognizable offence".

Provisions Relating to Arrest

There are various restrictions and liabilities that accrue when an offender is placed under arrest. His liberty is curtailed by way of confinement. He is expected to remain confined under the watchful eye of a guard or sentry. He is denied the privilege of putting on complete uniform as he is not allowed to wear his belt or other accoutrements. He is not permitted to carry arms.

Irrespective of the authority which orders the arrest, there is no denying the fact that there is a loss of face and reputation for the offender. His image gets sullied. Such a damage is almost always irretreivable. Normally a person under close arrest is detained in the unit quarter guard. The Defence Services Regulations, para 508, lays down that, "men undergoing rigorous imprisonment will be confined separately in the quarter guard or cell as far as possible and in no case two prisoners are to be confined in the same cell.

They will always be under the observation of a sentry. If a prisoner is admitted in hospital, a sentry will, if considered necessary be posted over him". Therefore such detention ipso facto assumes a form not very different from solitary confinement.

There is a definite need to examine whether or not it would be more humane if the circumstances and offences are clearly spelt out to lay down when it should be obligatory to place an offender under arrest. Undoubtedly the existing provisions appear to be harsh and stringent which warrant a relook. It should also be considered in all fairness whether or not these are as liberal as those laid down on the civil side to govern the detention of under-trials. In the case of Kishore Singh Ravinder Dev V State of Rajasthan; AIR 1981 SC 625, the Supreme Court had remarked that, "solitary confinement is justified only in extreme cases of compelling necessity for security of other prisoners or against escape after complying with rules of natural justice".

There is another angle to it which assumes significance from human rights angle. An army man under custody forfeits all pay and allowances for every day while he is in custody. There are statutory provisions in this regard as laid down in Army Act Secs 90 and 91. In the Indian context, where the husband is usually the only bread winner, his family is hit very hard when he is placed under arrest.

Mode of Arrest

Regulations para 392 further lays down that an accused person will be placed under close arrest during his trial by court martial. As long as the trial is in progress, the accused continues to remain under arrest. The mode of arrest does not change when he has to meet his lawyer or interview his witnesses. At times he is ordered to be handcuffed. It would be interesting to note that the Supreme Court had ruled that with regard to the hand-cuffing of the under trials, "the nature of the accusation should not be the guiding criterion. The clear and present danger of his escape or breaking out of the police control (to be substituted with military custody in our context) is the determinent. The only circumstance validating hand-cuffing of an under trial can be that there is no other reasonable way of preventing his escape in the given circumstance.' It is a constitutional mandate that no prisoner is to be hand-cuffed or fettered routinely or merely for the convenience of the custodian or courts".

In light of the foregone there is a case for review of the provisions relating to arrest. Apparently there is little jurisdiction for each and every accused person to be placed under close arrest, prior to and during his trial by court martial. What about mode of their confinement ? Space permitting, two or more prisoners should be lodged in the same cell unless there are special reasons to resort to the contrary.

Under the prevailing rules, an accused cannot claim to be assisted or represented by a lawyer during the hearing of charge or when the evidence is being reduced to writing. The existing provisions of the Army Act and the Army Rules do not provide for a friend of the accused to assist the offender in any meaningful manner at the stage of summary of evidence. Even at a stage when the matter is being processed for disposal by way of a summary trial under Army Act Sections 80, 83, 84 and 85 or during trial by summary court martial an accused cannot claim a right to be represented by a counsel or a defending officer. Further, the accused has been given no right to object to the court.

Legal Aid

The system for providing legal aid to the accused persons needs a reappraisal so as to provide him better opportunities to prepare his defence. This assumes importance due to certain cogent reasons. Firstly, the powers to award punishment given to a commanding officer are quite substantial. He can award rigorous imprisonment upto one year besides dismissing an offender from service. Thus, he can not only deprive a soldier of his employment but can also curtail his liberty for twelve months. Moreover, a dismissal in this manner usually dis-entitles an offender for any subsequent job under the Government or public sector undertaking. Therefore, the stakes are quite high for an accused when he is marched up to his commanding officer and, hence, the need to allow him legal aid. Thirdly, during most of their service span, army personnel usually serve in remote places and inhospitable terrain away from the civil population. At such places there is no legal aid easily forthcoming because there are no lawyers available close by. Even in those cantonments where a few counsels do reside they are not well versed in procedures of military law. Moreover, the soldiers can financially ill afford to engage them.

The accused persons are also at times handicapped because of ignorance of local language spoken by such lawyers. There is no legal aid inbuilt in the system which is available to a soldier at the pre-trial stage. What is the legal thinking in this regard which should guide us ? In a landmark judgement in the case of Khatri V State of Bihar; AIR 1981 SC 928; the Supreme Court had dwelt on the issue of right to free legal aid to poor or indigent accused who are incapable of engaging lawyers. "State is constitutionally bound to provide such aid, not only at the stage of trial, but also when they are first produced before the Magistrate or remanded from time to time. Such right cannot be denied on the ground of financial constraints or administrative inability or that the accused did not ask for it".

Tonight the Army going to get
a taste of Chemical Warfare.

YOU LOOK SO BEAUTIFUL ROZY, HOW OLD ARE YOU?
WELL! I AM 'PERPETUALLY' 19.
YASEEN

Under the prevailing system in the Army, for cases sought to be tried by summary court martial, an accused can be assisted by any person called "friend of the accused". This friend comes into picture only after an accused has been remanded for trial by SCM. In other words, the accused is without any expert legal aid at the state of investigation by court of inquiry when his character or military reputation may be at stake and provisions of Army Rule 180 having been invoked. Same is the case during preliminary investigation by way of hearing of charge and when summary of evidence is being recorded. Thus, till the time when actual trial commences, the so called "friend" is no where on the scene. Secondly, even when he comes into the picture, his role is limited because he is not a lawyer. As such he is not qualified to undertake the task assigned to him. Even the role played by him is quite limited. He cannot put questions to any witness or address the court. Therefore, he has little effectiveness and utility in the defence of the accused.

Constitutional Provisions

Fundamental rights enshrined in our Constitution are akin to human rights. Let us examine the constitutional provisions in the above regard. Clause (2) of Article 22 provides a safeguard for a person who is arrested. According to the same he shall not be denied the right to consult and to be defended by a legal practitioner of his choice. This clause postulates that there is an accusation against the person arrested against which he should be enabled to defend himself by engaging a lawyer of his choice. In order to effectuate this right properly and reasonably, it is necessary that the accused is allowed the facility to consult his lawyer in total privacy and confidence.

Our Supreme Court has held that the lawyer's service constitute an ingredient of fair procedure to a prisoner who is seeking his liberation. Free legal service to the poor and needy is an essential element of any reasonable, fair and just procedure. As pointed out above, the obligation to provide free legal service to a poor accused arises not only when the trial begins but also when he is produced for the first time before a Magistrate. In our context, it would mean at the stage of hearing of charge.

Access to justice is everyone's human right. Article 39A, a revolutionary contribution, indicates that "the State shall, secure that the operation of the legal system promotes justice, on an equal opportunity and shall in particular, provide free legal aid, by suitable legislation or schemes or in any other way, to ensure that opportunities for securing justice are not denied to any citizen by reason of economic or other disabilities. In light of the aforesaid, it would be desirable to re-examine the provisions contained in military laws so that legal aid can be easily availed by the army personnel involved in disciplinary cases.

Speedy Trial

Speedy trial as such is not a specific fundamental right. The Supreme Court has held that a delayed trial is not necessarily an unfair trial and a trial cannot be quashed on the ground of delay.Nevertheless a fair trial implies a speedy trial. No procedure can be reasonable, fair or just unless it ensures a speedy trial for determination of the guilt of such person. No doubt the disposal of disciplinary cases in the armed forces is normally speedy but the Army Act does not guarantee specifically any right to speedy trial. No hard and fast rule has been framed to indicate the maximum time it would take to complete the investigation process and commence the prosecution. There is no provision prescribing the maximum period for which an accused can be kept in custody awaiting trial. On the other hand, speedy trial is implied to be an integral and essential part of the fundamental right to life and liberty enshrined in Article 21 of our Constitution. Long pre-trial confinement of a soldier jeopardises his individual liberty.

Article 22 (3) of our Constitution prescribes that a person arrested and detained in custody is to be produced before the nearest Magistrate within a period of twenty four hours of his arrest excluding the time necessary for the journey from the place of arrest to the Magistrate's court. It thus ensures that a judicial mind is applied immediately to the legal authority of the person making the arrest and regularity of the procedure adopted by him.

In actual practice, it is not uncommon to come across accused persons who languish in custody awaiting commencement of their trial for the reported offences. In the army soldiers were at times kept locked in unit quarter guard cells for much longer period than the maximum prison sentence which could be awarded to them on conviction for the offence of which they were accused. Such a state goes against the basic tenets of human rights of being presumed to be innocent till proven guilty. Sometimes disposal of cases by courts martial gets delayed due to various reasons. These unhealthy trends should not be allowed to persist. To ensure speedy finalisation of cases it would be desirable to take all necessary steps including suitable augmentation of the cadre of the JAG Department so as to increase the legal and judicial resources.

Seen in the wider perspective of keeping the requirements of Army discipline in mind the military legal system would emerge as one which is quite sympathetic to the army personnel. However, Military Law like other laws is not a stationary monument. It has to be a dynamic and pulsating system which can effectively help the fighting forces to retain their discipline and enhance high morale. Therefore, it would be desirable to make necessary improvements in the existing legal provisions so as to keep them vibrant, alive and meaningful.

10

Legal Awareness for Army Wives

"There is no task before India which can compare with that of women's education. With five hundred men, the conquest of India might take fifty years; with as many women, not more than a few weeks. Perfect womanhood is perfect independence."

Swami Vivekananda

Soldiering is a full time profession. It calls for complete sacrifice, dedication and involvement of the troops towards the service. To achieve this a soldier needs to be made free from domestic worries. An Army man burdened with family problems will not be able to whole heartedly devote himself to the duties assigned to him, and more so in battle. The need for happiness, peace and satisfaction of a service family warrants no emphasis. An Army wife comes to play a pivotal role in the life of her husband. She can accomplish this task only if she is aware about the service routine. Knowledge gives rise to confidence and satisfaction whereas ignorance is the harbinger of fear, uncertainty and discontentment. It is, therefore, essential that the Army wives should be educated about their rights and privileges as well as the service conditions of the armed forces.

Human rights include Woman's rights. Gender justice is integral to social justice. While acknowledging the concept of equality of sexes as enshrined in our Constitution, the Supreme Court had held in the case of Yusuf Abdul Aziz V The State of Bombay; 1954 SCR 930 that Article 14 is general and must be read with other provisions which set out the ambit of fundamental rights. Sex is sound classification and although there can be no discrimination in general on that ground, the Constitution itself provides for special provisions in the case of women and children.

A large number of Army wives belonging to soldiers of infantry and other regiments hail from tribal areas and are illiterate. Supreme Court had opined in the case of Madhu Kishwar V State of Bihar; (1996) 5 SCC 125, "Women from time immemorial suffered discrimination and social inequalities and made them accept their ascribed social status. Among women the tribal women are the lowest of the low. It is mandatory, therefore, to render them socio-economic justice so as to ensure their dignity of person so that they may be brought into the mainstream of the national life".

The State is bound by the fundamental right proclaiming equality of sexes. But how would such equality of opportunity be translated in reality ? Possession of such a right is hardly of any meaning for girls hailing from the sub-educated and backward strata of society. Therefore, the primary need springs up to arrange for education and work towards female literacy. Efforts have been made in various cantonments under the aegis of AWWA (Army Wives Welfare Association) to organise classes for the army wives under "Nari Shiksha" schemes. AWWA is the only organised agency working for the cause of army wives, widows and their children on a national basis. AWWA and its counter part in other two services are purely non-governmental welfare organisations engaged in charitable and social activities.

Initially the thrust of such drives had been intended to be mainly directed towards eradicating illiteracy. However consequent to the gradual rise in the level of female literacy and due to social inhibitions these attempts at basic education managed to receive only a limited response. There is a pressing need to properly identify and select the disciplines on which desired knowledge should be imparted to the wives of the service personnel.

Issue of Practical Relevance

It is felt that the main thrust of awareness campaign to be launched by AWWA should be to increase knowledge of army wives about issues of practice relevance to them. It would be pertinent to advise the wife of a newly married soldier to ascertain whether the casualty return for her marriage has been published. She is to be told that it is only after such notification that a newly wed comes to acquire formal status as the wife of her husband. Otherwise, she may not get the benefits entitled to a next of kin. There was an instance where a military officer died under mysterious circumstances and the post mortem examination conducted by the army medical authorities attributed the death to extensive burns. The Supreme Court expressed pain at the utterly irresponsible conduct of the authorities and granted a compensation of rupees six lakh as well as family pension to the widow and also the children allowance in that case of Charanjit Kaur V UOI; AIR 1994 SC 1491.

There have been numerous cases where a soldier has abandoned his first wife and contracted a second marriage. What can the first wife do in such a case ? To cope up with such an eventuality, suitable awareness needs to be created about the legal rights and remedies available to such a helpless spouse. In a case of this nature if she had found out whether the official records contained her particulars as the legally wedded wife of her husband perhaps her plight would have been different. In a certain case after the death of a Naik of the Army, a dispute arose for the retiral benefits between two women both of whom claimed to have been married to him. The court decided the matter in favour of the one who was shown in the service record to be the legally wedded wife. She was held to be prima facie entitled to receive the dues including the family pension. The decision in this case of Gurdip Kaur V UOI; Punjab & Haryana High Court CWP No 7539 of 1993 is trend setting.

The wives should be told that as the years roll on the birth and particulars of each child should be duly reflected in the documents of her husband by way of personal occurences.

The wives of Junior Commissioned Officers and other ranks need to be suitably educated about the necessity for documentation matters pertaining to nomination and Will. They should be explained the reason why their husband needs to make a nomination. They would in turn advise their husbands to specify Next of Kin (NOK) for various purposes such as bank accounts, provident fund, pension, Army Group Insurance and other terminal benefits etc.

Financial Management

As part of basic financial management, an army wife should be made familiar with the procedure to open and operate an account in a bank or post office. She should also be explained how to fill a money order form. As part of the financial awareness, she should make herself abreast about the salary and other allowances paid to her husband. She should be made aware of the provisions which provide facilities for regular despatch of a part of his salary by way of family allotment. She must know that while on active service, or after the out break of a war, her husband can arrange regular remittance of money to her by way of such "family allotment". If she is informed about such provisions, the impact of ever looming fear of uncertainities would be considerably minimised.

Most of the house wives are totally dependent upon their husbands financially. What can a wife do when the husband does not send her money. The figures relating to the cases for grant of maintenance in the recent years are on an ascending graph. Army wives and specially those of the other ranks ought to be educated about the provisions relating to maintenance and the procedures to apply for the grant of the same.

The military service carries with it usual hazards involving outdoor activities and risks associated with handling weapons. Instances of unfortunate deaths, accidents and injuries are not uncommon in military life. An army wife has to be made mentally robust to cope up with such a tragedy. It would be in the interest of the ladies if they are apprised that suitable facilities exist for grant of disability pension, attendent allowance and special family pension to the victim of the mishap or to the family members.

A service wife has to frequently undertake journeys on leave,when going to join her husband or otherwise. At times she may have to move long distances without being escorted by her husband. The armed forces provide the facility of train journey at reduced fare. She should be explained the procedure for obtaining a railway concession form or how to get a warrant exchanged and thereafter arrange for the rail reservation. A concession is similarly allowed by the Indian Airlines on their domestic flights. It is essential that the wives are made known the entitlements of the families for treatment in military hospitals, both as an out-door and in-door patient.

Various Entitlements

Married accommodation is not easily available for military personnel. At times an army wife has to stay alone when she acquires the status of a separated family. During such times she may have to stay all by herself in a cantonment or in a house allotted to her in a civil area. Under such conditions she cannot do without visiting military hospital, schools, ration shops or canteen. To cater for such an eventuality she must be advised to note down and disclose necessary particulars about her husband like personal number, rank, account number, name of unit and sub unit, identity card number, place of posting and names of Commanding Officer etc.

Whether staying with or without her husband she should not depend upon him for minor errands. She could be explained the duties and location of various offices and agencies concerned with routine services so that she can approach the MES complaints cell, MI Room, ration stand, military police and Station Headquarters etc.

Of late, consumer protection laws have come to play a dominant role in the civil life. Instances may occur warranting lodging of a complaint against a gas agency, grocery shop or petrol pump etc. A service wife should be able to handle such a situation. To a large extent, service personnel have to depend on military canteens run under the aegis of the Canteen Stores Department (India). Although it is a monopolistic seller, yet the wives should know that they can forward their complaints regarding the items purchased by them from the CSD (I) Canteens.

Who is going to organise education on such matters. The army wives have to look after themselves. In addition, the officers of the Judge Advocate General's Department can be associated, where required, to play an important role to educate the army wives on the above topics. They may be assisted by the senior members of the AWWA. Classes on these subjects should be mainly directed towards the wives of the Junior Commissioned Officers and the other ranks. However, it should surprise none to find that even officers' wives are not adequately aware of these matters. As such they too would stand to benefit from such a drive. It is suggested that lectures on the above mentioned topics need to be organised on unit or station basis.

Instructions could be imparted by way of question and answer sessions. The venue and forum for such could be talks at the AWWA sessions or the family welfare meets. Suitable use can be made of leaflets and hand-outs printed in Hindi or other local languages and distributed to participants. To make the programmes more interesting proper use could be made of video films, charts and slides prepared for such topics.

11

ADR for Speedy Disposal of Court Cases Pertaining to Armed Forces

"People must help one another, it is nature's law."

Jean De Law Fontaine

The heavy back log of pending cases before the judiciary in our country has prompted various measures which are being examined to reduce the arrears of work. One of such proposals currently in discussion is called the Alternative Dispute Resolution (ADR). Urgent need has been felt to adopt and promote this practice for settlement of domestic and international disputes. A five-day training workshop for ADR practioners was held during August 1996 at Vigyan Bhawan which was presided by the then Chief Justice of India, Justice A M Ahmadi. The recommendations and report of this meet have put across some valuable suggestions to cut down the long list of undecided legal cases.

Dire necessity for promotion and extension of ADR exists amongst various legal disciplines in the country. Such a conclusion was understandably reached when it was unambiguously realised that the judicial courts alone were not in a position to tackle the entire burden of legal disputes. Consequently, alternative modes such as arbitration, mediation and negotiation are being accepted for achieving settlement of disputes.

While explaining the rationale to adopt negotiation as a mode as against public auction or invitation of tenders, the Supreme Court observed in the case of Sachidanand Pandey V State of West Bengal; AIR 1987 SC 1109 thus, "There may be situations where there are compelling reasons necessitating departure from the rule but then the reasons for the departure must be rational and should not be suggestive of discrimination. Appearance of public justice is as important as of bias, jobbery, or nepotism".

It is a common knowledge that the Government is one of the biggest litigants in our country. Various ministries and departments of the Central Government are involved in court cases as respondents, petitioners and appellants. The total number of legal cases being contested by the Defence Ministry and the Armed Forces Headquarters run into more than a lakh. It is also known that the rate of disposal of these cases does not indicate any downward trend. There are numerous reasons which contribute to delay in finalisation of these cases.

The prevailing procedure for the defence of these suits, based on the existing government orders and regulations of colonial vintage is not only time consuming but results in avoidable expense to the exchequer. Decision to contest each suit is generally taken at the apex level of Government of India or Service Headquarters and the process itself involves delay. The concerned officers are usually hesitant to concede even reasonable and genuine demands projected by the originators of the suits. Once a decision is taken to contest a suit, difficulties are observed in obtaining records from far flung offices for finalisation of replies to be submitted before the courts. Shortage of law qualified officers makes it difficult for units and formations to handle legal cases effectively. On the other hand, Government advocates are usually found to be unaware of the service laws and requirements of military exigencies. Consequently they are unable to suitably protect the interests of the Government.

Delay in finalisation of such cases cause undue hardship and misery to the aggrieved litigants who may finally succeed and get the relief after years. Secondly, it results in a heavy burden on the exchequer due to the expenses of litigation. Thirdly, it keeps the field commanders tied down to court battles and takes them away from their primary responsibilities. Lastly, every case decided against the Government indirectly invites strictures from the courts and adverse media publicity for the Government. There is thus a considerable scope for adoption of ADR as a method for settlement of legal cases within the armed forces. This practice can be usefully followed in cases of different types which need to be identified.

Personnel Issues

One of the areas where ADR can be put to use relates to personnel cases. Close on the heels of increase in female literacy and break up of joint families, incidents involving grant of maintenance allowance and plural marriages have shown a marked increase over the recent years. In a large number of such cases delay is caused not only due to vested interests of one of the parties but at times also because of ignorance and mis-apprehensions existing on the part of service personnel. The subordinates harbour fear about impending loss of service, military reputation or likely award of punishments to them. Hence, these individuals tend to delay the process and indulge in protracted correspondence before the final awards are made relating to grant of maintenance by the competent authorities. To cut down unavoidable wastage of time, manpower and resources, it is suggested that attempts should be made to finalise conflicting claims in these cases promptly by way of negotiations or mutual discussions. An ADR Cell should be created at the level of each formation headquarters such as Divisions or Areas to amicably resolve such cases. Assistance of the local AWWA (Army Wives Welfare Association) may be sought to protect the interest of semi-literate wives and children. Needless to say, desired amendments in the provisions of the statutes would be required in this regard.

Cases relating to pensionary awards, family pension and disability pension occupy a centre stage in the statistics relating to pending court cases. In almost all such cases, the Controller General of Defence Accounts (CGDA) are cited as one of the respondents. Lack of desired inter action between the formations and the CDA often results in incomplete replies being filed on the part of respondents and consequential delay in resolving the same. Past experience has shown that generally the courts tend to sympathise with the pensioners or helpless next of kin or with the disabled soldiers who appear before the courts as petitioners to seek redressal of their grievances. Considerable delays are experienced in compliance of court orders granting relief to the petitioners. Such legal skirmishes do not usually conclude in the first encounter. Usually the finance and accounts department mechanically advise recourse to file appeal against such orders. After prolonged legal battles in which appeals are always filed by the aggrieved parties before the higher appellate forum, the cases manage to reach final settlement. This too is an area where ADR can be usefully taken recourse to.

Disciplinary Cases

Disposal of disciplinary cases by way of courts martial is expected to be prompt. But generally it is not so. There can be no dispute that discipline must be maintained at all costs. It is also agreed that while upholding discipline, the Army should not adopt cost effective attitude. However, there are cases where ADR may be put to use for example, when a trial on a charge of attempted rape or misappropriation of funds takes almost two years to conclude, the outcome is a poor solace to either the victims or the protagonists of discipline. Disposal after two or three years of a case on a charge of outraging modesty with the award of "reprimand" to the accused appears to be travesty of justice. It cannot be said that the system has succeded in upholding discipline in such cases.

It would be far more appropriate to introduce into our legal system the American practice of "plea bargain". Recently it came to notice that women serving with the US Air Force were being accused in increasing numbers for court martial on adultery charges. When the Air Force was considering court martial of First Lieut Kelly Flinn, the country's first female B-52 bomber pilot charged with adultery for her affair with a married civilian and with fraternisation for having sex with an unmarried *enlisted man, Air Force Secretary Sheila Widnall announced that she would consider letting Flinn resign with an* "honourable discharge". It makes more sense to enter into a dialogue with the accused who may put forth a plea of guilty to say negligence rather than misappropriate of funds. Further, prompt disposal by way of award of "severe reprimand" or "forfeiture of seniority" etc. should be preferable to almost the same punishment by a court martial after a trial that drags on for a couple of years, or at times more.

Next sphere where ARD can be made use of pertains to cases filed by the contractors belonging to Military

Engineering Service, Army Welfare Housing Organisation and supplies to the Army Service Corps. These cases generally involve issues relating to Law of Contracts. In all such cases substantial financial interests of the Government are usually at stake. Undoubtedly, the parties to the dispute would benefit and stand to gain if these matters are mutually resolved by ADR without delay. The process of arbitration do not appear to be inspiring much confidence. Negotiations with fair and impartial attitude may succeed in breaking the deadlocks over conflicting claims. Panel of competent arbitrators and umpires need to be drawn up to settle these cases by experts of proven integrity.

Disposal of MACT Matters

At any given time, there are normally dozen of inquiries in progress in any command zone with regard to traffic accident cases. Not infrequently loss of lives or injuries are caused in such incidents. Such cases drag on for years because of want of eye witnesses, civil police officials who would have handled the incidents and post mortem reports. Sometimes military drivers are found blame worthy. Resultantly, Station Headquarters at various cantonments are saddled with the burden of scores of MACT cases to defend. Considering the liberal and sympathetic attitudes of the existing compensation tribunals towards the victims of mishaps, it would be prudent to shift to ADR for disposal of such cases, to the satisfaction of various parties.

Another sphere is the cases pertaining to acquisition or grant of compensation by the defence estate department. Disputes take place over the resumption of bungalows in cantonments, dehiring of houses in possession of the defence department or taking over of lands for the armed forces. Thousands of cases of such nature are pending in various courts all over the country. These matters too can be settled by means of mediations and negotiations.

A pragmatic and bold approach is the need of the hour to settle the ever increasing backlog of court cases and thereby enable the field commanders to devote their attention and undertake their primary tasks and operational necessities.

12

International Humanitarian Law
Perspective and Challenges in 21st Century

> "Liberty lies in the hearts of men and women. When it dies there, no constitution, no law, no court can save it. No constiitution, no law, no court can ever do much to help it".
>
> Judge Learned Hand

The theory that freedom of the individual must take second place to the security of the State cannot be easily ignored. The notion of legitimate democratic governance is only plausible in a country where the security and safety of the State is not endangered. Viewed in that light, at times the natural justice may take second place to national security. Despite the same, a large number of nations had agreed centuries ago that the vanquished in war need to be protected from slaughter and suffering.

Humanitarian laws were evolved and instituted as a permanent system for humanitarian relief. Rousseau wrote in his *Contract Social* in 1762 with regard to Humanitarian Law "these principles are not those of Grotius, they are not founded on the authority of poets, but they flow from nature of things and are founded upon reasons".

Humanitarian law relates to the right of particular categories of human beings principally the sick, the wounded, prisoners of war - in particular circumstances i.e. during periods of armed conflicts. Modern conventional texts are based on the principle that a number of basic human rights are so fundamental that they must be respected at all times and even in periods of armed conflicts. This constitutes the basic theme of the International Humanitarian Law (IHL).

Humanitarian law is one branch of the law of human rights and human rights afford the basis for IHL. Humanitarian law comprises of two branches - Law of War and Law of Human Rights.

At times it is said that the IHL has remained mainly a code of conduct for the nations to adhere. Violations in its provisions are often cited to support such a contention. It is pertinent to note that the very fact that the rules of war exist on paper is a great step forward; the next one will be to ensure that they are applied. The new model, though incomplete, does at least indicate the routes to be avoided; as well as the main thoroughfares that it would be best for the States to follow. Admittedly the progress of the contemporary law of war has been unsatisfactory and imbalanced. The main problem today is not one of framing the required legal provisions but rather of their enforcement. In other words, it is no longer a question of agreeing on the rules but, by police action, of seeing that they are observed.

What is required in the context of humanitarian law is to further strengthen the system to look after the interest of, and secure the humane treatment of - the sick, the wounded, prisoners and other victims of armed conflicts. Promotion of such task is being undertaken by the International Committee of the Red Cross (ICRC).

Ensure Implementation

Humanitarian considerations constitute the inspirational base for rules relating to Law of War. Geneva conventions have been framed on the bed rock of humanitarian values. Such considerations do not, however, by themselves amount to rule of law. These considerations led the former UN Secretary General to once opine that "While the International Committee of the Red Cross and certain organisations play a most useful role, there would be pressing need for measures to improve and strengthen the present system of international supervision and assistance to parties to armed conflicts in their observance of humanitarian norms of international law. These measures, based on what already exists, should be regarded as complementary rather than competitive". It is, therefore, essential that a permanent system for humanitarian relief needs to be strengthened and made more effective.

Istanbul Declaration of the 21st International Conference of the Red Cross held during 1969 had announced, "That the universally recognised general principles of law demand that the rule of law be effectively guaranteed every where". Ways and means are to be, therefore, devised to ensure implementation of such expectation so that the text of the declaration does not merely remain empty words on paper.

There are various challenges before the world community in the matters of humanitarian laws. The foremost need is to ensure that flagrant violations of the IHL should attract stern action from other States. Perceptible forms of exerting pressure need to be introduced e.g. censure by the world bodies, withholding of military aid and arms sale etc. But at the same time hasty actions would be counter productive and hence, should be avoided. For this purpose, international fact finding missions undertaken by impartial and expert observers in the field may have to be more frequently resorted to.

Collective action by the member countries of the ICRC will continue to be an effective deterrent against offending nations. The words of Spinoza recorded way back in 1677 are no doubt still pertinent, "whereas freedom or inner strength are the virtues of the individual, a State knows no other value other than its own security". Hence, the vital need for the member countries to act united. It is also hoped that States in the distant future will continue to be guided by humanitarian values for fear of being censured, denounced, criticised and in extreme cases, delegitimized by a majority of other members of the world community.

Promote Acceptability

The "Geneva Conventions Act" was legislated in 1960 by Indian Parliament to give effect to the four Geneva Conventions of 1960. The enforceability of the Geneva Convention Act 1960 was examined by the Supreme Court in the case of Rev Mons SFXDR Monterio V State of Goa; AIR 1970 SC 329. It held in para 15 thus, "The Conventions are not made enforceable by Government against itself nor does the Act give a cause of action to any party for the enforcement of Conventions. There is only an obligation undertaken by the Government of India to respect the Conventions regarding the treatment of civilian population but there is no right created in favour of the protected persons which the Court has been asked to enforce".

In the coming years, another task for IHL would be to devise ways and means to promote its acceptability amongst the States. The past records indicate that out of 166 States invited by the Swiss Federal Council for the 1974-77 Conference held in Geneva, only 124 attended the first session. This number came down to 120 for the second session held in 1975, further dropping to 107 for the third conference (1976). Finally, only 109 countries attended the last session held in 1977. These diminishing figures indicate a progressive decline in the number of countries coming forward for participation in IHL deliberations. This tendency further appears disturbing from the fact that only 102 States came ahead to sign the final Act of the conference on 10 June 1977. Reasons for such a trend need to be analysed. It is hoped that the furture will usher greater acceptability to the IHL movement by the countries of the world.

Another significant observation indicates that the offers of the services of the International Committee of the Red Cross have been accepted in approximately only half the armed conflicts which have occured after the setting up of ICRC. It would be desirable that the humanitarian law movement proceeds to achieve greater acceptability amongst member nations. What are the reasons that the States shy away from letting the ICRC do its noble and humanitarian task ? Efforts need to be made to analyse the reasons for such a response and to further propagate the significance of the ICRC so that its good offices can be used during all armed conflicts.

Decades ago, IHL activists had decided to come to the rescue of slaves. The Geneva Convention of 1958 on the Law of the High Seas had provided in its Article 13 that the High contracting parties will prevent and punish the transport of slaves in their vessels. It further stressed that any slave taking refuge thereon shall be made free. This indeed was a laudable step.

Similar action needs to be taken with regard to protection of hostages. The recent decades have seen the increasing trend of hostages being taken by the militant groups to force the opposing side to accede to their illegitimate demands. It is also done to generate media focus. In context of Kashmir militancy in India, this malpractice came in the lime light with the kidnapping of Dr Rubayya Sayed and Doraiswamy of Indian Oil Corporation during the early nineties. Thereafter four western tourists who were on a visit to the valley and were taken hostage. They still continue to be held in captivity. The ill treatment of such innocent persons cannot be allowed to continue. Would IHL remain a silent spectator ? The international community needs to take stock of this practice and discuss ways and means to intervene.

The framers of this branch of law have shown foresight by including in the text of the covenants derogation of various articles relating to humanitarian law that may be anticipated. It has been provided that the words "in time of public emergency which threatens the life of the nation" is wide enough to include a time of war. However, it is felt that in order for a derogation to be lawful, the public emergency must be "officially proclaimed". It may imply that in situations of undeclared war or civil strife, no derogation is permissible in the absence of an official proclamation of a state of emergency, so that all the rights proclaimed in the covenant must then continue to be respected. The next millennium will test the adequacy and competence of the international forums to restrain and contain the violence in internal armed conflicts.

Need for Re-Appraisal

There are some aspects of the existing law that need a reappraisal. The first protocol has laid down that "the parties to the conflict shall accept without delay an offer which may be made by the ICRC". There is, thus, a definite obligation on them to admit the good offices of the ICRC and, if necessary, to accept it as a substitute. There is a need for a similar unequivocal corresponding provision in the second protocol relating to internal conflicts. In the coming decades, there does not appear to be any possibility of such internal conflicts coming to an end. Hence, there is a definite requirement that the ambit of the second protocol needs to be suitably expanded so as to include internal conflicts also.

Another problem which needs to be tackled by the IHL relates to the relief against damage and loss caused during the rebellion in a country. Each State has, as a part of its inherent sovereignity, the right to quell armed rebellion within its territory. However, under the prevailing scene, rebellion has not been made a concern or a violation of international law. Therefore, a solution has to be found with regard to provision for relief to the victims of inter-state armed conflicts. Similarly, while the humanitarian treatment of war victims has received a major focus of the IHL, something substantial needs to be done with regard to the victim of violence unleashed during terrorism.

Situations of internal disturbances and tensions such as riots, isolated and sporadic acts of violence and other incidents of a similar nature, not amounting to armed conflict, have been left out of the purview of protocol 2. It is hoped that the world bodies will address themselves to this issue with a view to at least provide shelter and relief to the victims of such destructive activities.

Besides probability of nuclear strikes and a spate of conventional battles, the emerging decades may witness increasing instances of state sponsored terrorism. Such situations are more likely to develop in Third World countries where stable governments have yet to be established as a matter of practice. IHL has to come up with concrete suggestions to meet these challenges by providing adequate care and protection for the victims of disturbances of such kind.

Another sphere to which IHL has to give its attention is to streamline and regulate the codifications giving extra ordinary powers to the States to deal with situations involving recourse to weapons for maintenance of internal security. For example, in India we have had Terrorist and Disruptive Activities (Prevention) Act, Disturbed Areas Act, Maintenance of Internal Security Act, Defence of India Rules, Armed Forces (Special Powers) Act besides the Code of Criminal Procedure and the Indian Penal Code. Under a multiplicity of legislations, all giving substantial powers to men in uniform, while deployed in situations of armed conflict, the likelihood of the wounded and the sick finding themselves totally neglected and deprived of their dignity and personal rights cannot be ruled out. In such a back drop what needs to be done ? Firstly where ever possible a single comprehensive Act may be framed and secondly such proposed Act should be so designed as to be in tune with the basic manifesto of the IHL.

International intervention in what were hitherto internal matter of States has gradually come to be accepted by and large if not universally, as legitimate and even necessary. Human rights, per se, have engaged the attention of the peace activities. Dr Butros Butros Ghali, the then UN Secretary General of the UNO, had placed human rights at the top of the UN's agenda, along with peace and security and sustainable developement. During his opening address at the World Conference on Human Rights at Vienna on 14 June 1993, he had called upon the countries to make basic rights of human-kind into instruments of national policy. He called for the adoption of human rights as a common language of humanity that would bring about global understanding and bind the world into a single community. Similar action is required with regard to the basic rules of international humanitarian law.

Hague Convention XII of 1907 had provided for the establishment of an international prize court. Articles 4 and 5 of this Convention related to the contingency of neutral nations claiming rights against a foreign State before the court. However, no provision has been made with regard to rights of a foreign State to claim compensation from the group of people belonging to another country. To illustate, country "X" may wish to claim compensation from a group of people (say "Y") belonging to the country "Z". IHL would do well to come forward with a solution to this requirement.

An annual report is submitted by the Human Rights Committee and the General Assembly via ECOSOC (Economic and Social Council) about its performance. In a similar fashion a system of international supervision could be introduced whereby reports of IHL violations and breaches by the governments would be compiled and be available for examination in the like manner.

Armament Industry

International Humanitarian Law will have to face the challenge of curbing the lethality of modern nuclear weapons. The destructive power of such weapons is so enormous that it obliterates the distinction between enemy combatants and non combatants. Neutral foreigners have to suffer nuclear fall out and the ensuing environmental damage. Hence, according to universal morality, nuclear war can never be the lesser evil. No nation can be morally justified in protecting its own existence by means which do serious harm to neutral nations. Nor does universal morality justify a nuclear armed strike in response to a nuclear first strike. It is sheer vengeance and there can be no human right to revenge.

The ensuing decades have to bring forward means to put a squeeze on the armament industry. For successful and any meaningful adherence to the IHL, the killing zone of the area weapons has to be reduced and curtailed. The weapons with bigger destructive potential need to be curbed. But will the concerned industries take to it willingly ? Certainly not. Therefore, in the coming years, we have to make concerted efforts for diversion of defence industry towards manufacture of productive and peaceful items. Shift from destructive to peaceful manufacture has to be attained by means of a sustained drive by the signatories to the IHL.

So far participation in the activities of IHL seems to have remained the sole responsibility of the signatories to the various protocols. It is only the governments and a few NGOs like National Red Cross Societies who have been working to promote IHL, with the notable exception of the ICRC. It is equally noteworthy that armed conflicts everywhere always bring enormous destruction and disturbance. Normal civil life, trade and commerce are all disrupted. The economy of the countries involved is put to severe stress. It is, therefore, imperative that the corporate sector should come forward to impress upon the need for awareness and implementation of international humanitarian law. It is hoped that the immediate future will see the business world joining together to face this challenge.

Another direction in which IHL has to traverse relates to economic pressurisation. Paragraph 2 of Article 4 of the United Nations Convenant on Civil and Political Rights lists certain sacrosanct rights with regard to which no derogation may be made. Relevant for the purpose of this article are the right to life, the prohibition of slavery and servitude, and the right to freedom of thought, conscience and religion. All such rights cumulatively imply the right to live with dignity and honour. If that be so, then the action in the recent past by some of the developed countries to grant the Most Favoured Nation (MNF) status or to impose economic sanctions is nothing but infringement of IHL on a collective basis. In this regard too the international community may wish to raise its voice.

IHL is not the monopoly or the concern of the elite class. It does not have to relate only to the affluent and highly educated sections of the member countries. Its meaning and importance has to reach the vast masses who may find themselves in the shoes of either the oppressor or the oppressed. In this context, it is disturbing that the propogation of this subject is confined only to English speaking people in our country. In the Indian sub-continent million of people who are not familiar with the English language are unaware of the message of IHL. The coming times would hopefully see dissemination of IHL literature in the different spoken languages of the world.

Induction of Professionals

Emerging decades will witness induction of professionals in the IHL area. Maximum violations and conversely adherence to the Law of War would be at the level of the individuals serving in the defence forces. This would be at various levels, be it a rifleman or a General commanding the troops in a theatre of war, or a group of men collectively manning a PW camp. Suitable education about IHL needs no emphasis. Who is going to impart this training ? There is a crying need for specialists who are well versed with wars and weaponry, provisions of Military Law and also display instructional aptitude. There is an acute shortage so far of such experts which are expected to be identified and recruited in the coming years.

Who is going to monitor humanitarian law violations ? IHL can be enforced only when its violations are noticed, reported and corrective actions taken. This calls for effective supervision which cannot be left to the capabilities and interest of the individuals and manual capabilities of impartial observers. Therefore, what is needed is the resort to electronic means which may detect and record acts of violence. Greater reliance needs to be placed on communication satellites and other surveillance measures.

Adherence to the IHL to a great extent is to be carried out by the Armed Forces. An integrated approach is

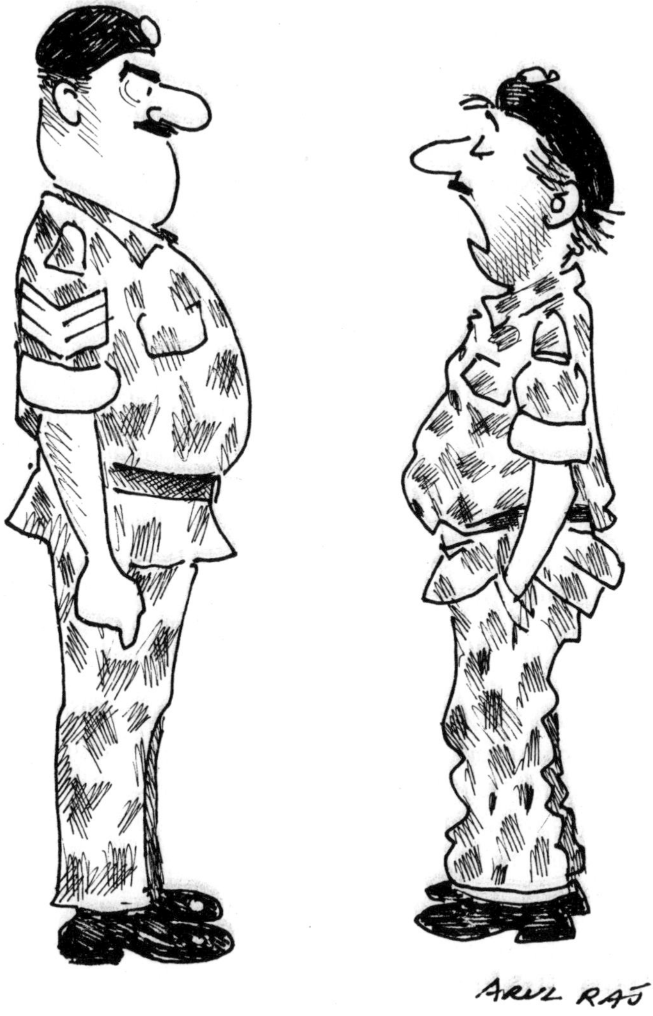

What does the Army want -- Male
Fashion Models or dare devil Killers

warranted to achieve uniformity in the understanding and application of Law of Wars. Directorates of Military Training of the member States should address themselves to this task. Instructional capsules would have to be chalked out to train officers of different armies. Such programmes could be drawn to be run on the pattern of E-IMET (Expanded International Military Education and Training) courses being run by the US Naval Justice School at Newport, Rhode Island by the US Navy.

Training

It has been well recognised that no nation possesses an absolute monopoly on the formula for basic democratic principles, human rights, international humanitarian law and military justice. Therefore, it would be prudent to design training with a view to custom tailor each course to fit current country specific legal and military situations. Such inter action would undoubtedly build strong and lasting relationships and contribute to common shared goals of regional stability.

We need to espouse those military values which are a source of consistent strength because they preclude an army dissipating its strength on wanton acts of destruction and do not create a requirement to defend gains because of enduring hostility from the civilian population.

The words of Jose San Martin, "The nation does not arm its soldiers for them to commit the indecency of abusing said advantage by offending the citizens who sustain them through their sacrifices" are still relevant today in this context. It is hoped that abiding faith in the spirit of the Geneva Conventions and determined efforts to keep them progressive would go a long way in lessening the sufferings of those who are unfortunate to undergo the miseries of war.

13

IHL in the Context of Wars of National Liberation

> "Make haste in doing good; check your mind from evil; for the mind of him who is slow in doing meritorious actions delights in evil. Should a person commit evil he should not do it again and again, he should not find pleasure therein; painful is the accummulation of evil. Should a person perform a meritorious action he should do it again and again; he should find pleasure therein; blissful is the accummulation of merit".
>
> *Dhammapada 116-18*

International Humanitarian Law relates to the rights of particular categories of human beings principally, the sick, the wounded, prisoners of war. Secondly this law is applicable in particular circumstances, i.e. during periods of armed conflict. IHL comprises two branches namely the law of war and the law of human rights.

The last four decades have seen an increase in the instances of violent conflicts of inter state or intra state nature. Such armed disturbances have been called by different names in various regions of the world at different times. They have been termed as sponsored terrorism, civil war, insurgency, militancy, guerilla movement, proxy war, armed rebellion, irregular war, low intensity conflict or organised resistance movements.

A number of countries today are plagued by border disputes, ethnic tensions or violent clashes brought about by separatist, religious and fundamentalist groups. Fellow countrymen are ridden with internal dissensions over issues that relate to differences over caste, creed, communal, racial or religious identities.

Violent means adopted by differing factions often result in bloodshed and destruction, the effects of which usually transgress international boundaries. After the outbreak of hostilities in such situations, the political parties in power obviously make all out efforts to regain and retain their control over the government. Corridors of power in such countries are averse to any outside interference in what they perceive as their internal affairs. They are also sensitive to the reactions of the world forums and human rights organisations.

What is the attitude of the authorities in power against those who happen to be on the opposite sides in these conflicts ? Though care is taken so as not to label the opponents as "enemies" but at various times and in different places they have been called as anti national elements (ANEs),terrorists, guerillas, rebels, militants or insurgents. Yet various countries have deployed their military forces armed with all their conventional weapons to combat, control and at times crush such opponents who yet ironically are not addressed as "enemies".

There may well be a conflict between humanitarian considerations and the ones based on security. Such a matter came up before the court in State of J&K Versus J & K High Court Bar Association; 1994 Supp (3) SCC 708. The dispute was between the need to supply food, water, medical and sanitation facilities to the innocent hostages detained by militants in a shrine on one hand and to flush out the militants on the other. What was the proper course in such a case ? Taking both aspects into consideration, the Supreme Court issued directions for satisfying the requirement of innocent hostages in the specified manner

An appraisal of the record of help sought by the civil administrations from their armed forces would unearth useful material needed to study ways to enhance the scope for the role of ICRC to provide help to the victims of armed violence in situations which do not classify to be called as international armed disputes. For the purpose of this study, let us call such situations as insurgency.

Magnitude of Problem

How frequent is it that a State has to requisition the help of its Armed Forces to restore normalcy in a strife torn portion of its territory ? In the context of India, according to the official figures, such situations are not rare. During the two decades, 1950-70, the Army's aid to restore law and order was sought on approximately 476 occasions. Between January 1979 to December 1980, on 64 occasions which works out to every eighth day. From 1980 to 1984 the Army was employed on approximately 369 occasions, that is once every fourth day. No doubt that in a large number of such instances the situation had not deteriorated to such as extent as to be equated with insurgency. Yet if mishandled and allowed to be further aggravated in the Indian scenario as also elsewhere, these instances have the requisite potential of degenerating into troublesome consequences in the form of insurgency.

Insurgency is a situation where an alienated minority is agitating for a cause and political and administrative mishandling has turned it into an insurrection and consequently taking the form of terrorism and guerilla warfare.

In the context of insurgency situations or wars of national liberation, the international community has so far confined its concern largely to two parties. These are the two sides engaged in combat viz the security forces operating on behalf of the administration on one hand and on the other side the militants who have taken to arms. There is a third party which remains mostly neglected and overlooked. Reference is made here to the helpless civilians who have to suffer as a result of the disturbances caused. They are uprooted from their homes and have to migrate to safer pastures as refugees. Their homes are destroyed and as a result they find themselves unsettled. It is these neutral civilians who often get trapped in the cross fire and thereby sustain injuries and are at times killed too.

There is no end to the misery of such civilians. Their trade and livelihood are adversely affected. Education of their children gets disrupted. While in the disturbed areas they live in the constant fear of violence and death. In recent decades Bangladeshis, Afghans, Vietnamese, Rwandans, the Boat People and others have all faced such miserable plight. Armed militants have been responsible for numerous human rights abuses including torture, rapes, killing and taking of hostages.

There is little doubt that such destruction is caused as a result of armed conflicts. The victims and the culprits, sufferers and oppressors are all human beings. Care needs to be taken to ensure that the rights of the weaker side are not ignored and violated upon. The militants often succeed in winning sympathy of the media. But human rights cannot be the privilege of terrorists alone.

What is required in the context of humanitarian law is to build a system that can look after the interests of and secure humane treatment of all the parties involved that is the militants, the security forces and the neutral helpless civilians.

How can this be achieved ? The advocated option is to gear up the media projection with a view to expose the plight of the common man. On one hand, the depiction of the atrocities committed upon the innocent civilians may attract wide condemnation. On the other hand, it may bring in revulsion in the minds of common man at the violent and brutal means adopted by the insurgents. It would also keep in check high handedness and careless actions of the security forces. They would have to be on guard due to the risk of being criticised or exposed for their excesses. Thirdly, it would generate interest and admiration at the painstaking efforts of relief agencies like the ICRC.

Hostages

Action to provide succour to the victims of armed violence need to be taken in accordance with the provisions of the Geneva Conventions. ICRC operates within its laid down charter. Guidelines adopted by the ICRC to define the framework for its action are no doubt sacrosanct. In their formulation care had already been taken to ensure that they do not prove to be too restrictive. There has been gradual expansion in the scope of IHL activities over the years. To begin with, its mandate was confined to international armed conflicts. Thereafter it was extended to situations of internal violence. Now it has come to encompass within its reach humanitarian initiatives which the State agencies and the institutions may take in the wake of pressing humanitarian needs. Such an option may be taken up even when the violence has not reached an alarming scale.

The ICRC has shown commendable interest in the field of care of prisoners of war. However, due attention needs to be focussed on the plight of hostages. Experiences gained during last two decades is evidence of ground realities where there is still scope for relief operations to be undertaken. Amendments to various Conventions could be carried out to cater for suitable procedures which facilitate obtaining information about the identity of hostages. Moreover news should be communicated about their whereabouts and their physical condition to their home countries. Despatch of parcels to them besides furnishing of medical supplies should be provided for.

One of the seven and the first fundamental principles of ICRC as contained in its preamble is "humanity". It stipulates that the movement "endeavours, in its international and national capacity, to prevent and alleviate human suffering wherever it may be found. Its purpose is to protect life and health and to ensure respect for the human beings" (emphasis given). In this regard, it would be significant to enlarge the scope of the word "health" in its contemporary sense. The word does not mean a mere subsistence ? Doesn't it imply in the above context that the IHL movement is required to safeguard against ill health ? Where does ill health begin? A bottom line should be drawn so that certain minimum acceptable standards can be laid down. Violence or attacks against "health" should relate to not only damage in the physical sense but also hurt caused to the civilian population and hostages by mental trauma or due to threat of violence.

Refugees

In the decades bygone, millions of people were exposed to danger and terror in our sub-continent. They were driven to such a stage that they had no option but to run as refugees from Bangladesh and more recently from the Kashmir valley. They abandoned the States of their origin due to threats of violence. A purely legalistic study of the IHL doctrines may suggest that any intervention by the world agencies had not yet been attracted in their cases. It is in such situation that the spirit behind the regulatory provisions deserves more importance than a plain literal text of the words used. It may be said that their plight fell short of the limit and consequently intervention by the IHL did not come to apply. In this context, it would be worthwhile to appreciate the spirit of the provisions which gives a clue to their objects. The legal definition of the word "assault" indicates a reasonable apprehension about use of force. The law of crimes as contained in the Indian Penal Code makes an act of assault also punishable. Viewed in a similar vein the connotation of the word "health" should be suitably interpreted to include even an apprehension of the threat of violence which may endanger health of the victims.

The Supreme Court has held that right to life is integral to right to live. While expanding the scope of Article 21 (right to life), it said that right to life includes the right to live with dignity. Therefore, a progressive and liberal view needs to be taken to propose introduction of suitable amendments to the IHL provisions in this context. It is hoped that the proposed International Criminal Court of Justice will provide an effective forum for adjudication of related disputes, particularly in view of its advisory jurisdiction.

14

Role of the Army Educational Corps in the 21st Century

"Education has been called the technique of transmitting civilisation. In order that it may transmit civilisation, it has to perform two major functions: it must enlighten the understanding, and it must enrich the character."

Nani A Palkhivala

Some very momentous decisions have been taken in the field of human resource development in the Army during the course of the last decade. It was during this period that the Sports College was set up in the place of the erstwhile P T School; Sports Medicine and Hospital Administration came to be recognised as new disciplines in the study of medical sciences by the Armed Forces; an Institute of Military Law was set up at Kamptee. Rather than confining themselves to the management of Army Schools, Army Welfare Education Society treaded on new vistas by venturing into opening of Army Institute of Technology, Pune; the Army Institute of Hotel Management at Bangalore; and the Faculty of Management Studies at Jabalpur. Induction of women officers was started in various arms and services. Departing from the earlier practice of training courses being designed to the officers upto the rank of Brigadiers only, a regular training capsule for the Major Generals came to be introduced at College of Combat, Mhow.

The above healthy and welcome trends are indicative of an earnest desire to develop human resource in the Armed Forces. Education is an on going process. The famous Jurist Sri G S Pathak was firmly of the view that, "the greatest boon that can be conferred on the common man would be imparting of instructions through educational processes in what his rights are. A realisation of his rights will raise his stature". The Supreme Court had expressed its views in this regard clearly in the case of Maharashtra State Board of Secondary and Higher Secondary Education V K S Gandhi; (1991) 2 SSC 716, "Education nourishes intellectual advancement to develop dignity of person without which there is neither intellectual excellence nor pursuit of happiness. Education thus kindles its flames for pursuit of excellence, enables and ennobles the young mind to sharpen his/her intellect more with reasoning than blind faith. "

Viewed in the above context, there is a need to carry out a reappraisal of the role and scope of Army Educational Corps (AEC). This requires heart searching and puts forth some probing questions. While at the threshold of the 21st Century, can we afford to sit idle and let the changing situations overwhelm us? Is'nt it time to critically revaluate and give new meaning to age old concepts ? Whether or not the deployment pattern of all support and ancillary services of the Army needs to be reshaped after first formulating our goals and strategies? Can we say that we have become educated enough as to make redundant the need for AEC? Is there no further need for education? Should the AEC be rechristened as Corps of HRD ? An attempt has been made in this article to present a monologue on the conceptual changes required in the role and scope of AEC in the next century.

In the peace time scenario, the role of AEC resources has to be primarily targeted to educate and equip the soldiers so as to bring them to a common takeoff level. Such a task is of paramount importance in the present context when it is seen that the candidates recruited from different states possess educational standards which are not identical. While the academic criteria prescribed for induction into the Army may have been raised but this has not in any manner improved the quality and level of literacy. It is, therefore, felt that at the training centres, stress has to be laid on academics so as to bring the recruits to the desired level of knowledge in Hindi, English, Mathematics and Science. Unless such an approach is rigorously adopted we may find that the recruits and young soldiers present themselves to be miserably incompentent to match up with the fast changing technologies associated with the modern warfare techniques.

AEC personnel have certain inherent assets in the form of instructional skill and competence. They have had exposure to higher education in the colleges and the universities. Due to late entry in service, their level of maturity is higher than their counterparts in other arms and services. Past experience has shown that AEC JCOs/NCOs are a valuable asset to the units due to their higher knowledge base, professionalism, instructional skills and other abilities which make them suitable for any challenging task in the units and formations.

Topics of Contemporary Relevance

Since the AEC staff has been traditionally responsible for handling classroom training, they are qualified and experienced to impart instruction. Soldiers look upon them with respect. Hence, AEC instructors should also be asked to educate the young soldiers not merely on the academic subjects but on a variety of topics of contemporary relevance such as financial management as applicable to them, ill effects of the use of drugs and alcohol, dangers of AIDS etc. Benefits and spin offs from such a proposal would be well justified for the organisation and the individuals. It would also increase general awareness and confidence of the men,thereby enhancing their employability.

The glaring shortages in the officer cadre having more than 12000 deficiencies in the junior ranks can be offset to an appreciable measure if the channel of Army Cadet College and Special Commission is successfully harnessed. The Corps should also be associated in training of the senior NCOs and JCOs of all arms and services for pre-commission coaching and the SSB preparation so as to raise their preparation level for grant of commission as an officer. The inhouse expertise of the AEC staff can be gainfully utilised for coaching about group discussion, interview and other tasks.

Another area in which officers and other ranks of AEC need to be increasingly made use of is to impart education in various Sainik Schools, Military Schools and Rashtriya Indian Military College, Dehradun (RIMC). This would enable these Institutions to have advantage of the service of uniformed personnel in the manner befitting for residential schools. Secondly, the students themselves would get proper motivation by the instructors hailing from such disciplined forces being part of the regular army rather than being taught by the civilian teachers who not infrequently have been found to indulge in trade union activities thereby setting a bad example in front of their pupils. Similarly making use of such staff at the NDA and OTA extensively is suggested in view of the obvious advantages.

A large number of officers are availing study leave facilities every year. However, the number of officers who can be spared to be away from units and formations on a full time basis on study leave is limited in view of service constraints. Hence, a need emerges to encourage self study with guidance from regional centres, manned by AEC personnel. There is another area which may call for deployment of AEC cadre. Himachal Pradesh High Court in its judgement dated 24 December 1993 in the case of Havildar SC Bagri V Union of India had held that denial of the right for study leave to an NCO is highly discriminatory and violative of Article 14 of the Constitution of India. In light of the same, the possibility of study leave provisions being thrown open to the JCOs and men in future cannot be ruled out. Nevertheless to meet their aspirations for improving their educational horizon and for its further widening, a thought need to be given by introducing suitable courses to be run through the medium of correspondence. The Army could follow contemporary example of distance learning and system of open universities to that end.

Information Technology

Setting up a university for defence education is a crying need. Such a university could seek recognition as "deemed university" or otherwise. In fact various faculties of such a university are already existing at Pune in the form of Faculty for under graduates (NDA), Engineering (CME), Medicines (AFMC), Technology (AIT), Theology (INI) and so on. The main advantage of such a university would be that it would be able to standardise the education syllabus for servicemen hailing from across the length and breadth of the country. Secondly it would provide legitimacy and recognition to our existing army courses by granting them status of certificate, diploma or degree. Thereby it would enable improved opportunities for resettlement to the future ex-servicemen qualified with certificates and diplomas awarded by such a university. B F Skinner had said that education is what survives when what has been learnt has been forgotten. If and when such a university of defence education is set up,

TRANSIT CAMP
TIMINGS
AGREED SAAB! SAME 'MENU' EVERYDAY, BUT THIS IS TRANSIT CAMP, HERE OFFICERS KEEP CHANGING, WHILE 'MENU' REMAINS THE SAME.
YASEEN

the AEC personnel would provide the necessary nucleus for its organisational and administrative structure both for teaching and non teaching posts.

Army cannot lag behind in this era of information technology. Presently, we are drastically short of computer exposed/literate personnel at user unit level. The men have to be brought up to the level expected to assimilate and grasp computer uses. War games have to be devised of varying standards to tone up their reflexes and professional knowledge standards. Tie up with agencies like APTECH is the demand of the day.

Requirement to learn foreign languages will not only continue to exist but increase in the coming decades. Requirement of staff trained in library management will also be there. Use of information technology and the latest teaching aids should be assigned to the AEC instructors to shoulder the above responsibilities efficiently.

How do we make out the optimum utilistion of these professionals during active hostilities? The earlier suggestion of AEC personnel being given the responsibility of Nuclear, Biological and Chemical Warfare cell at formation headquarters needs to be given a more detailed thought and concrete shape. Media management should be entrusted to them and they ought to be trained for the purpose by the experts in media communication. They should also be assigned the duties concerning psychological operations. They could in addition be utilised to carry out interrogation at Prisoner of War cages besides relieving and assigning General Staff in the operations room. Their services would further be in great demand for augmenting controlling staff in other duties along the lines of communication including tasks related to refugees.

Low Intensity Conflicts

In the prevailing situations as existing in the Valley and North East, AEC staff need to be skillfully employed to gain psychological advantage by organising classes for the children of the locals. Their services can be of immense practical demonstrated concern of the Army towards the younger generation. Handling of the media, both electronic and print, should be assigned to them. They are specially suited for the same due to their proximity to formation headquarters, access to libraries and being part of the General Staff.

A voice has been raised at times by certain quarters to do away with the Army Educational Corps or to carry out major reductions in their manpower. The saving, thus accrued, in terms of number of personnel may surely allow raising of a few battalions but that would alone not be a battle wining decisive factor. However, the consequential impact on the Indian soldier qualitatively will be disastrous which would only be felt by the coming generations.

Army Education Crops has played a significant role in training Unit Education Instructors (UEI) courses conducted at the AEC Training College and Centre, Pachmarhi. While a large number of the commanders and commanding officers realise its utility and are full of appreciation, a few tend to hold an opposite view due to enhanced educational qualifications for a General Duty (GD) soldier to matriculation. Such a view is indicative of ignorance of ground realities. It is felt that qualified UEIs are free of stage fright and may be utilised by the units for a variety of duties. Being familiar with the language of the troops, such instructors are useful as a trained multi-purpose manpower to handle varied jobs. Over the years, UEIs have been exposed to new methodology of communication skills. Syllabus for such a course with slight modifications would entitle them to appear for Bachelor of Teaching degree successfully. It may, therefore, be necessary to review its course contents and QR periodically.

With the induction of latest technology and modernisation of defence forces, the strengthening and redeployment of AEC cadre is more pertinent in our organisation where human resources development is fundamental to create best soldiers in all aspects. The aim should be to strive for making educational efforts fulfill the organisational training needs while not losing sight to satisfy the individual aspirations. I would conclude with the words of Nani Palkhivala, "when new dangerous tremors are working their way through the subsoil of our national life, it is only the character and dedication of the young generation that can ensure the survival of freedom." The word "soldier" may be substituted for "generation" in our context.

15

Military Law Approach to the Prosecution for Violations of IHL

Provisions of Geneva Conventions are meant for universal application. They come into play and assume special relevance in times of war or other armed conflicts which are of a non-international nature. IHL provides for the penal repression of certain violations. Complete and faithful adherence to the Conventions could be expected by infliction of effective punishment on those violating them. International penal responsibility is inconceivable without an obligation on the part of the State parties to the said IHL treaties to bring the authors of acts constituting grave breaches before their own courts. Military Laws contribute to International Humanitarian Law (IHL) in a significant way. Those engaged in armed profession would frequently find themselves in situations that warrant implicit need to adhere to the Conventions and Protocols. Used with discernment, especially for preventive purposes, such provisions present undoubtedly effective measures.

The men in uniform are governed by Military Laws applicable to their countries. There is a case for humanitarian laws to be translated and connected to the jurisdiction governing armed personnel. The importance of dissemination of laws of war to the men in uniform warrants no emphasis.

Overview

The violations of IHL, for the purposes of this paper, may be classified under three heads. Firstly, we have grave breaches of the Geneva Conventions and the additional protocol. Then there are violations which, however, do not constitute as grave breaches. Lastly, breaches of Conventions other than Geneva Conventions.

The sanctions for grave breaches of humanitarian law are not self-executing. War crimes trials are acceped as authoritative interpretations of the laws of war. Individuals have international duties that transcend the national obligations of obedience set forth buy different States. Is there an excuse available for non adherence? An immunity for violating the laws of war is not available on the plea of having acted "in pursuance of the authority of the State if the State in so authorizing action moves outside its competence under international law."

English common law has influenced the legal systems of Commonwealth nations. It may be the heredity of common law or the vestige of colonialism that the Geneva Conventions Act of the common law countries have identical features. A study of the uniform pattern as adopted by these countries is helpful for a clear understanding of the criminal sanctions available under national legislations.

The criminal legislations of these countries enacted pursuant to the Conventions are based on universality of jurisdiction. Australia, New Zealand, Botswana, Canada, Ireland, Kenya, Malaysia, Papua, New Guinea, Nigeria, Seychelles, Singapore, United Kingdom, Zimbabwe, India,

Malawi and Uganda all provide for extra territorial application.

Secondly, persons triable under the military laws of the respective countries by courts martial or military courts are not triable under Geneva Conventions Acts. The reasons are logical. Members of the armed forces are tried for military and civil offences by courts martial and not by ordinary courts of the country. If a member of the armed forces is guilty of "committing grave breaches" he is not to be tried by the ordinary courts but only by courts martial.

Thirdly, the personnel of the armed forces of a State that has not ratified Protocol I (like India) have no legal obligation to comply with non-customary provisions of that Protocol.

Offences other than War Crimes

In a broader sense the term 'war crimes trial' may denote any judicial proceedings, domestic or international, in which war crimes, crimes against humanity or genocide have been committed. Serious crimes like genocide or crime against humanity or aggression all undoubtedly need to be firmly curbed. Having regard to violations of IHL other than the Geneva Conventions, it is noteworthy that some of the Conventions are self-executing. In such cases, the relevant laws are competent to deal with their violations. Confusion continues to exist over the definition of crimes against humanity and their relationship to war crimes and aggression. However, the perpetrators of an act of aggression would generally be amongst those individuals who have the necessary authority or power to be in a position potentially to play a decisive role in committing aggression. These people can be designated as "leaders", "architects" or "organizers". Individual responsibility for such a crime is intrinsically and inextricably linked to the commission of aggression by a State. An individual, whether as a leader or an organizer etc. can only participate in that aggression.

A crime of genocide would refer to an act of killing or violence to destroy, in whole or in part, a national, ethnic, racial or religious group. According to the UN Convention of 1948, genocide is a crime under international law which may be committed in time of peace or in time of war. This would often require some involvement on the part of high level Government officials or military commanders as well as their subordinates. It may be committed by constitutionally responsible rulers. This requires an intent that may be difficult to establish.

Crimes against humanity would consist of acts which would be committed in a systematic manner or on a large scale. These crimes would take place when instigated or directed by a Government or any organization or group. Crimes against humanity would reckon in context of an aggressive war. One of the essential pre-requisites indicates that such acts would be committed in a systematic manner meaning thereby pursuant to a preconceived plan or policy. It would exclude a random act which did not take place as part of a broader plan or policy. The second condition is that the inhuman acts should have been committed on a large scale. It would imply that the acts are directed against a multiplicity of victims.

Perpetrators of such undoubtedly crimes deserve penal actions. High level civilian officials of the Government or the political leaders are not subject to the jurisdicion of the military law. Therefore, the military law approach would not be an appropriate option for dealing with these crimes. Such persons would fall within the category of accused for whom the trigger mechanism of the future International Criminal Court would be activated. It is expected that the said Court would be able to effectively address the prosecution for the crimes of aggression, genocide and those against humanity.

The scope of this paper has been confined to war crimes that includes grave breaches enumerated in the Geneva

Conventions and Protocols. It would also address itself to non grave breaches of the Geneva Conventions. An attempt has been made to discuss the practice concerning military law approach to prosecutions for IHL violations in the Indian context. The presentation further provides a broad view of the situations emerging elsewhere and particularly in common law countries with regard to domestic law alternative to deal with the aforesaid crimes.

Constitutional and Legislative Framework

Having due regard to the Indian practice for imposing sanctions for violations of IHL breaches, it is imperative to be aware of the existing legislative framework. Relevant provisions of the Constitution of India, the Army Act, Geneva Conventions Act, Protection of Human Rights Act, Armed Forces (Special Powers) Act and the Commission of Inquiry Act present the basic statutes for this approach.

Certain provisions as contained in the Constitution of India are relevant to the subject matter of the topic under discussion. The same have been listed in Table 1.

The Indian Constitution has envisaged scope for imposition of martial law under certain extraordinary situations. Such a contingency could arise during a period of armed conflicts. Article 34 of the Constitution of India empowers the Parliament to make an Act of indemnify to cover illegalities committed during the operation of Martial Law. According to this article, Parliament may by law indemnify any person in the service of the Union or of a State or any other person in respect of any act done by him in connection with the maintenance or restoration of order in any part of India where martial law was in force or validate any sentence passed, punishment inflicted, forfeiture ordered or other act done under martial law in such area. Although martial law has never been imposed in any part of India ever since the Constitution came into existence, yet during such an eventuality, indemnify may be conferred on any person or group of persons by the Indian Parliament by enacting a suitable provision in that regard. It was held by the Supreme Court of India that the effective martial law in India cannot be imposed so long as the right to life and liberty guaranteed by Article 21 of the Constitution of India is not taken away. Apex Court and High Courts can entertain cases under their constitutional powers in the event of violation of Article 21 and these rights cannot be given away to the control of military authorities or tribunals. (*C S Rao Vs The Supreme Commander; AIR 1980, Andhra Pradesh 172*).

Judiciary is one of the powerful organs of the State. The Supreme Court of India is the Apex Court of the country. The law declared by the Supreme Court is binding on all Courts. However, it is a noteworthy feature of Indian Constitution that the Supreme Court has no power of superintendence over any judgement, determination, sentence or order passed or made by court martial. Similarly High Courts, though invested with power of superintendence over all courts within their territories, have been invested with no power to interfere with decisions of military tribunals in respect of matters placed within their jurisdiction of the law. In this manner courts martial appear as the tribunals armed with effective and exclusive powers to deal with violators of military law.

The Supreme Court under Article 32 and the High Courts under Article 226 have been nevertheless armed with the power of judicial review over courts martial. It was held that such courts can grant appropriate relief if Fundamental Rights have been denied, or if there has been jurisdictional error or any error of law apparenton the face of record. (*S N Mukherjee Vs Union of India; AIR 1990, Supreme Court, 1940*)

Any person who feels aggrieved by any action on the part of the State can seek legal remedy. The Armed Forces constitute one significant instrumentality of the State. Right to secure legal remedy is also available against actions contemplated under military law approach. Article 39 A of the Constitution provides that the State shall secure that the operation of the legal system promotes justice, on the basis of equal opportunity. It shall, in particular, provide free legal aid by suitable legislation or schemes or in any other way, to ensure that opportunities for securing justice are not denied to any citizen by reason of economic or other disabilities. Section 304 (1) of the Criminal Procedure Code, 1973 contains suitable provisions to render free legal aid.

Article 51 of the Constitution concerns promotion of international peace. The relevant extract of this article states: The State shall endeavour to:

(a) promote international peace and security;

(b) maintain just and honourable relations between nations;

(c) foster resoect for international law and treaty obligations in the dealings of organised people with one another.

Article 51(C), however, does not mean that an international Convention is *ipso facto* enforceable upon ratification. It has been held that in the absence of contrary legislation, municipal courts in India would respect rules of International Law. But if there is any express legislation contrary to a rule of International Law, Indian courts are bound to give effect to Indian Law. The Supreme Court of India had held in the case of Jolly George Verghese and another Vs Bank of Cochin; AIR 1980, Supreme Court 470 that, "The basic human rights enshrined in the International Covenants. . . . may at best inform judicial institutions and inspire legislative action within member State, but apart from such deep reverence, remedial action at the instance of an aggrieved individual is beyond the area of judicial authority."

Army Act, 1950

The Indian Armed Forces are governed by the Army Act, 1950, Air Force Act, 1950 and the Navy Act, 1957. The Salient features of the three Acts are generally identical. Chapters 1 and 2 of the Army Act pertain to the application of military law and the definition of terms used in the said Act. Persons who once become subject to the Army Act remain so subject until duly retired, discharged, released, removed, dismissed or cashiered from the service. Section 4 of the Army Act enebles the provisions of the Act to be applied to any force raised and maintained in India under the authority of the Central Government, although the force may not be part of the Regular Army. It may also suspend the operation of any other enactment which may otherwise for the time being would have been applicable to the said force. Everyone who is permanently subject to the military law (except officers, Junior Commissioned Officers and Warrant Officers) is subject to that law by virtue of his enrolment. The principle underlying this provision is that no person should be permanently subjected to an exceptional and severe code like that contained in the Army Act without a definite act on his part. Such an act e.g. enrolment is susceptible of easy proof from entries contained in the enrolment paper. Certain Fundamental Rights, for example, to form associations or unions and of speech and expression and assembly have been abrogated for the military men. Army Act Sec 21 provides for the restriction of certain Fundamental Rights which are otherwise conferred on every citizen under the Constitution.

Chapter 6 of the Army Act classifies under various heads and defines the military and civil offences. Offences of similar character are grouped together. The groups have, as regards military offences, been arranged in such an order as to emphasize their relative military importance. Sections 71 to 75 provide the scale of punishments which can be awarded by courts martial to persons subject to the Army Act. The Act provides that a court martial, subject to the limits imposed by the said Act upon its powers, may award a specified maximum punishment or such less punishment as is mentioned in the Act. However, it has to be in accordance with the scale laid down. A maximum punishment is only intended to be imposed when the offence committed is the worst of its class, or is committed by a habitual offender, or is committed in circumstances which require an example to be made. A penal deduction may also be imposed. This is, in principle, a deduction made as a penalty for an offence of which an accused has been convicted. It constitutes part or whole of his punishment.

Chapter 9 of the Army Act provides for various contingencies in which a military offender may be arrested by military and civil authorities.

Chapters 10 and 12 contain the principle provisions governing the convening, composition, procedure, revision and confirmation of court martial. It also lists certain provisions relating to jurisdiction of court martial and evidence. The Summary Court Martial is peculiar to Indian Army. This enables the Commanding Officer of a unit to convict and sentence military offenders and thereafter to issue a warrant for the execution of his sentence. They have proved peculiarly suited to the conditions of Indian Army and are now the tribunals by far the most frequently utilised for the trials of military offenders.

Chapter 13 provides for the execution of sentences which have been duly passed and, where necessary, confirmed. Elaborate provisions exist relating to suspension of sentence.

of imprisonment. In addition, Army Rules and Regulations have been framed which are in the nature of subordinate and delegated legislations. These further amplify and set out the procedure for maintenance of discipline and administration of justice in the Army.

Certain definitions as contained in the Army Act are relevant for the purposes of this study. The term enemy as defined in Sec 3(x) includes all armed mutineers, armed rebels, armed rioters, pirates and any person in arms against whom it is the duty of any person subject to military law to act. The term 'civil offence' has been defined by Sec 3(ii). It means an offence which is triable by a criminal court. The word 'offence' means any act or omission punishable under the Army Act and includes a civil offence. It is noteworthy that the word 'combatant' has not been defined in the Act, Rules or the Regulations.

Offences

Grave breaches specified in Conventions and based on wilful killing or causing serious injury to body or health may usually be made subject matter of a charge under the criminal law. So would be the case of unlawful deportation, unlawful confinement and taking of hostages. On the other hand, grave breaches in the nature of torture, inhuman treatment, biological experiments and destruction or appropriation of property that is not justified by military necessity may fall under the scope and definition of various military offences as listed under the Army Act.

Military offences have been listed under Sec 34 to 68 of the Army Act. The scope and purview of some of these offences would extend to cover a number of grave breaches. They could also cover non grave breaches of the Conventions and the Protocol. Table 2 lists out statement of offences as included in the Army Act which may be made use of to frame charges for violations of war crimes under certain situations.

The Army Act provides that breaking into any house or other place in search of plunder by armed forces is an offence under Sec 36(b) and punishable with imprisonment which may extend to 14 years if committed on active service and otherwise to seven years.

Military personnel undergo a training regimen that emphasizes above all the need to obey and not question military orders. However, reasonable orders can be distinguished from clearly aberrant ones. Sec 41 pertains to disobedience of a lawful command. It is to be noted that a subordinate is duty bound to comply with a command given by his superior officer, provided the command was in the first place lawful. There are certain clear ingredients of a command that go to make it lawful. Firstly, it must relate to a military duty. That means its disregard should have the effect to delay, prevent or impede a military operation. Secondly, it should be specific and capable of individual execution. Thirdly, it must have reference to a date and time. It should be justified by military, as well as by civil, law and usage. The command could be verbal or written. The plea that an impugned order was not a lawful command would be valid defence.

A commander who issues an illegal order is liable to be called upon to explain his conduct. He is responsible for his action whether or not his order was obeyed. On the other hand, a subordinate who obeys an unlawful command can have no valid defence if made simply on the plea that the order had emanated from his superior. It is noteworthy that generally the individuals that carry out the breaches of the IHL would not be exculpated at the international level by a plea of obedience to superior orders or absence of national legislation to that effect. This legal situation is sufficiently demonstrated by the Nuremberg and Tokyo trials held after the Second World War.

Section 53 of the Army Act declares that extortion by a member of armed forces is an offence punishable with imprisonment upto 10 years.

Oppressing a person, disturbing any fair or market, committing riot or tresspass etc. amounts to an offence under Sec 64(a) and punishable with imprisonment that may extend to seven years.

Any person who defiles any place of worhip or otherwise intentionally insults the religion or wounds the religious feelings of any person may be punished with imprisonment upto seven years. Such lapses would fall under Army Act Sec 64(b).

Commission of an offence against the property or person of any inhabitant or resident of the country in which serving is punishable under Sec 64(f) with seven years imprisonment.

Section 63 relates to any act or omission which though not specified in the Army Act is prejudicial to good order and military discipline. This offence is punishable with imprisonment that may extend to seven years. To secure a conviction under this section it needs to be proved that the act or omission was prejudicial both to good order and military discipline, having regard to the nature and to the circumstances in which it took place. An ommission to be punishable under this section must amount to neglect which is wilful or culpable. If wilful i.e., deliberate it is clearly blameworthy. Where applicable this section may be used to deal with offenders who are alleged to have committed grave or non-grave breaches of the Conventions or the Protocol.

Geneva Conventions Act

India was one of the first six countries in the world to ratify the Geneva Conventions in the year 1950. It is also a matter of record that the Army Act which is modelled on the pattern of the Indian Army Act of pre-independence era was passed and came into force on 22 July 1950. Subsequently, 10 years later the Geneva Conventions Act (Act VI of 1960) was enacted in 1960 and came into force on 12 March 1960. However, no changes or amendments were made to the Army Act after 1950 in so far as the Chapter of offences is concerned. It, therefore, makes it obvious that none of the grave breaches or non-grave violations of the Conventions were incorporated in the Army Act.

According to the Geneva Conventions (in short GC) Act, these Conventions form integral part of Indian law, Chapter II of the Act provides for punishment of offenders against Conventions. Grave breaches of the Geneva Conventions have been made punishable by Section 3 of the said Act. This section specifically and exclusively provides for trial of offenders who are accused to have committed grave breaches. However, the Act is silent about measures required to be taken for suppression of acts which are in the nature of non-grave breaches of the Conventions. Section 3(1) of the Act provides that if any person within or witout India commits, or attempts to commit, or abets or procures the commission by any other person of a grave breach of any of the Conventions he shall be punished with death or imprisonment for life or for 14 years depending upon the gravity of the offence. Section 4 provides that where an offence under the Act is committed by any person outside India, he may be dealt with in respect of such offence as if it had been committed at any place within India at which he may be found. This caluse would enable the Government of India to prosecute a person on the basis of universal jurisdiction as well as to ask for extradition by establishing jurisdiction.

Section 17 imposes a ban on the courts from entertaining any complaint unless it is filed by the Government or an officer of the Government specified by notification.

Therefore, an aggrieved party can request for prosecution only through the Government. If the violator is an agency of the Government like military personnel, it is unlikely that the government will make a complaint to the court against such violations. There is a definite case for amendment of this section so as to confer the right to make a complaint before the court to private individuals or their representatives or to impartial international organisations like the ICRC.

Case law exists on the scope and extent of remedies available under the above Act. Supreme Court ruling in the case of Rev. Mons Sebastiao Francisco Xavier dos Remedios Monterio V The State of Goa reported in AIR 1970 Supreme Court 329 is to be referred in this regard. The Court held, "The Act by itself does not give any special remedy. It does give indirect protection by providing for breaches of Convention. The Conventions are not made enforceable by Government against itself nor does the Act give a cause of action to any party for the enforcement of the Conventions. Thus, there is only an obligation undertaken by the Government of India to respect the Convention regarding the treatment of civilian population but there is no right created in favour of protected persons which the court has been asked to enforce." According to some experts, such an interpretation has rendered the incorporation ineffective.

Section 7 of the said Act is relevant for the purposes of this presentation paper. It relates to jurisdiction of Courts Martial. It provides, "The Army Act, 1950, the Air Force Act, 1950 or the Navy Act, 1957 relating to trial by court martial of persons who commit civil offences shall have effect for the purpose of the jurisdiction of Courts Martial as if this Chapter had not been passed."

Theoretically action with regard to violations of IHL could be initiated against the defence personnel under three modes. Firstly, under the criminal law of the land (domestic courts). Secondly, under the military law provisions. Lastely, by duly authorised international tribunals. Let us examine tha actual situation as existing in Indian context. GC Act is the relevant Statute in this regard. Its provisions are to be read against Section 69 of the Army Act which deals with civil offences. By virtue of this section any civil offence which is triable by a criminal court amounts to an offence under the Army Act.

Passage of Section 69 as relevant for the present discussion states - "Subject to the provisions of section 70, any person subject to this Act who at any place in or beyond India commits any civil offence shall be deemed to be guilty of an offence against this Act and, if charged therewith under this section, shall be liable to be tried by a court martial and, on conviction, be punishable as follows, that is to say:

(a) if the offence is one which would be punishable under any law in force in India with death or with imprisonment for life, he shall be liable to suffer any punishment, other than whipping, assigned for the offence, by the aforesaid law and such less punishment as in this Act mentioned.

(b) in any other case, he shall be liable to suffer any punishment, other than whipping, assigned for the offence by the law in force in India, or imprisonment for a term which may extend to seven years, or such less punishment as is in this Act mentioned.

Therefore, due to the insertion of Section 69, a person subject to the Army Act may be tried and punished if he is alleged to have committed any civil offence which is triable by a court martial under Section 69 of the Army Act. It, therefore, emerges that a trial by court martial of a person subject to the Army Act accused of having committed a civil offence can be envisaged under Section 69 of the Army Act. Section 69 itself provides for the trial of civil offences. A grave breach of the Geneva Conventions, if it amounted to an offence under any other enactment of the domestic law, could have been made subject matter of a trial by court martial. The offender could have been made to answer for his actions/omissions. Had Section 7 of the GC Act not been inserted in the statute, an offence relating to grave breaches of the Conventions would have amounted to a civil offence and thereby attracted trial jurisdiction under Section 69 of the Army Act. However, Section 7 of the GC Act has brought about a situation whereby trial by court martial of a person who commits civil offence cannot be held because of the legal position introduced by Section 7. Therefore, it would not be feasible to try a military person who is accused of having committed a grave breach of law of war within the meaning of the GC Act by a court martial. Of course he would be liable to be tried for an offence relating to the said breach if the same otherwise can be described as a military offence listed under Sections 34 to 68 of the Army Act.

With regard to non-grave breaches which do not qualify or amount to offences under domestic law, the same position would emerge as discussed above. Trial by way of court martial may be convened provided a charge can be framed under the Army Act. Similar position would be there under the Air Force Act, 1950 or Navy Act, 1957.

Military Law Approach

In general terms, no universal jurisdiction is recognized by military justice codes. Acts or omissions of military nature are to be reserved to be dealt by military justice statutes. The general approach of military law to violations of municipal law envisages subjection of defence personnel to the Army Act as well as the law of the land. Generally this is the statutory position in all Commonwealth countries. A person in uniform can be made answerable for a lepse which amounts to an offence under the Army Act. Alternatively, he is liable to trial under the local law which is applicable to all citizens. The domestic laws contain adequate provisions needed to resolve the conflict of jurisdiction which may arise when both the courts martial and the criminal court are competent to deal with an offender having regard to the nature of offence.

The position as existing in India, with reference to prosecution for grave breaches of the Conventions, is also analogus and some what similar. Military personnel are liable to face criminal proceedings under domestic law for commission of any offence within the meaning of Geneva Conventions subject to the legal position discussed. They can otherwise be brought to trial before a court martial provided that the charge framed against them relates either to an offence under the Indian Penal Code or the transaction falls under any of the military offences as included in Sections 34 to 68 of the Army Act.

Military Law approach, as outlined, is better suited to deal with prosecution for IHL violations. This is because of a number of advantages inherent to the system. Action under the Army Act can be resorted to for charges in regard to breaches that take place during civil wars, a course that would not be available under Geneva Conventions Act option. This mode can be equally utilised for breaches committed during operations which are not of an international magnitude or relating of IHL treaties like the 1954 Cultural Property Convention. Trial by *ad hoc* tribunals like a court martial convened solely to deal with an offender on a specific charge sheet is quicker. The accused is afforded suitable judicial guarantees to prepare and present his defence. He has greater confidence and faith in the fairness of the system where his peers constitute the court martial. There is a wide range of punishments from which suitable penalty can be inflicted upon him. Therefore this approach stands out as more convincing and competant to restore discipline and respect for the law amongst the troops.

However, military law approach has certain distinct disadvantages. Firstly, the system of courts martial does not have the benefit of judicial precedents of its past decisions. As a result the advantage of relying on its own rulings or earlier judgements cannot be made use of. There is no benefit of past precedents to guide subsequent legal tribunals. Secondly, while UK and some other countries have set up a Court Martial Appellate Court, a parallel tribunal is yet to be established for the Indian Armed Forces. Consequently, there is no opportunity available to an accused to put up a meaningful appeal providing a right of personal hearing against a court martial verdict. Thirdly, such an approach is not available to deal with non combatants who do not fall within its jurisdiction. Lastly, States are entitled by IHL to prosecute an alien national on their territory who has committed a war crime against alien nationals in other countries. However, this alternative can not be made use of in India if we depend on military law approach to prosecute offenders belonging to foreign armies. There is also a misplaced apprehension about protectionism. This aspect would be covered little latter in this presentation.

Investigation of Offences/Inquiry Procedure

All criminal proceedings entail an enquiry. This type of enquiry is prescribed in national legislation in India. There is a well defined procedure for investigation of offences at pre-trial stage. An inquiry can be conducted as shown in Table 3 under the procedures set forth in the Army Rules or by a commission set up under the Commissions of Inquiry Act or by way of a report demanded by the National Human Rights Commission.

Army Rules and Regulations provide for investigation of any incident involving discipline by way of a court of inquiry. Such an inquiry is a fact finding body. It may be convened by any officer who is commanding the forces at any level.

Rules of natural justice and judicial safeguards are duly observed. When military reputation of a person subject to the Army Act is involved at the inquiry then full opportunity is provided to such a person of being present throughout the investigations. The opportunity relates to cross examining any witness, making a statement and producing witnesses in defence of his character or reputation. The Regulations stipulate that the presiding officer should be senior in rank and other members atleast equivalent in rank to such a person. When so directed, the evident may be recorded on oath. The Court usually submits a report in the form of its findings and opinion which are recommendatory in nature.

National Human Rights Commission

National Human Rights Commission has been set up under the Protection of Human Rights Act, 1993. The Preamble of the Act affirms that it has been enacted for better protection of human rights and for matters connected therewith or incidental thereto. Section 19 of the Act specifically relates to procedure with respect to the armed forces. It provides that on receipt of complaints of violation of human rights by a member of the armed forces, the Commission shall either on its own motion or on receipt of a petition seek a report from the Central Government. After the receipt of the report it has two options. It may either decide not to proceed with the complaint or it may make its recommendations to that Government. The Central Government shall inform the Commission of the action taken on the recommendations within three months or within further time extended by the Commission. The Commission is legally bound to publish its report together with its recommendations made to the Central Government. It shall also indicate action taken by that Government on such recommendations. The Commission is required to provide a copy of the published report to the petitioner or his representative.

Third mode for inquiry is to make use of a Commission. An Inquiry Commission can be appointed by an appropriate Government under Section 3 of the Commission of Inquiry Act (Act 60 of 1952) for the purpose of making an enquiry into any definite matter of public importance. The Commission may consist of one or more members. It is invested with the powers of a civil court while trying a suit. It may examine witnesses on oath, require the discovery and production of documents. It may receive evidence on affidavit, requisition any public record and issue commission for the examination of witnesses and documents. It may also utilise the services of any officer or investigation agencies. On the basis of the report of the Commission it would be legally feasible to launch prosecution of persons who are alleged to have violated the applicable laws and regulations.

In this back drop, it would be pertinent to recall that Article 90 of Protocol 1 requires the setting up of a Fact Finding Commission to investigate grave breaches that are alleged and restore an attitude of respect for the Conventions and Protocols. Common Articles of the Conventions provide that "an enquiry shall be instituted, in a manner to be decided between the parties (I, 52; II, 53; III, 132; IV, 149). Any of the three modes available under domestic practice may be adopted to carry out an enquiry envisaged by the laws of war.

Disciplinary Action

Administration of criminal law justice through national courts is efficient and effective. The enforcement of International Humanitarian Law through domestic criminal sanctions may lead to its greater viability. Sanctions are important because penalties are an integral part of any sound legal system, particularly due to their deterrent value.

Depending upon the gravity of the offences, States could treat non-grave breaches to the Conventions or the Protocols as serious offences under their own penal legislation and go for imposition of criminal sanctions. Alternatively, trials for breaches other than grave breaches can be conducted in the ordinary disciplinary ways. Under the Conventions, the High Contracting Parties are obliged, inter alia to, take measures necessary for suppression of all acts contrary to the provisions of the Conventions other than grave breaches. (I, 49; II, 50; III, 129; IV, 146).

An offender belonging to the Armed Forces can be brought to trial under the normal criminal law. On the other ahnd, if it is decided to proceed against him under military law approach then there is a wide range of options available. These alternatives are either statutory or based on conventions, customs of service and, in one case, derive their authority from judicial precedents. Such an alternative can also be met by summary disposal provisions. The Protocol enjoins that with respect to their subordinates the military commanders are obliged to prevent and, where necessary, suppress breaches of the Conventions and Protocols. They are required to initiate steps for disciplinary action where so required (AP I, 87). Various modes available for taking action under the military approach are shown in Table 4.

The most commonly invoked option in the military approach is by way of courts martial trial. There are four types of courts martial, out of which most potent is a General Court Martial. It can be used to deal with any accused, irrespective of his rank who is charged with any offence, whether civil or military. If found guilty it can award him any punishment including death penalty. As discussed earlier the Supreme Court and the High Courts have no power of superintendence over courts martial verdicts.

The other commonly used mode is summary disposals. The officers commanding divisions and areas have been invested with the powers to deal with officers of the rank of Majors and below, or the JCOs and Warrant Officers, by way of summary disposal under Section 84 of the Army Act. If found guilty an accused can be awarded forfeiture of seniority or service for a period upto one year. In addition a penalty of severe reprimand or reprimand can be inflicted. Further, they can be awarded stoppages of pay and allowances to make good any loss or damage occasioned due to their act or neglect.

The commanding officers have been armed with the powers to dispose of summarily the case of a Non Commissioned Officer or other ranks. The relevant provisions are contained in Army Act Section 80. There are a wide compass of punishments out of which a suitable penalty can be chosen to be inflicted upon an accused and the maximum being upto 42 days of imprisonment and detention. These summary powers may be made use of effectively to meet the obligation cast under Protocol 1, Article 87 which enjoins military commanders to initiate disciplinary or penal action against violators of the Conventions or of the Protocols.

The Army Act also provides for recovery of penal deductions from the pay and allowances of the military personnel. Army Act Section 25 enjoins that pay of any person subject to the Act due to him as such under any regulation for the time being in force shall be paid without any deduction other than those authorised by the Army Act or any other Act. Relevant provisions are to be found in Sections 90 and 91. Deductions may be ordered with regard to every day a person is in custody or under suspension from duty on a charge for an offence for which he is afterwards convicted. These are meant to make good compensation for any expenses, loss, damage or destruction occasioned by the commission of an offence as may be determined upon conviction. Such deductions could also be imposed in respect of any sum required to make good any loss, damage or destruction of public or regimental property which after due investigation, appear to the Central Government to have been occasioned by the wrongful act or negligence on the part of an individual.

Yet another mode of action is by way of what is commonly known as administrative action. All persons subject to the Army Act hold office at the pleasure of the President who is empowered under Army Act Section 18 to remove any such person from service. No opportunity to show cause is required to be given prior to taking recourse to such action under the doctrine of Presidential Pleasure.

Another option available is to resort to Section 19 whereby the Central Government can terminate the services of any person subject to the Army Act for any lapse or misconduct. Usually the principles of natural justice are duly observed. The delinquent is afforded an opportunity to furnish reply against the contemplated action.

The customs of service cater for administration of reproof to a person whose conduct or performance so warrants. Commanders at various levels have been empowered to award censure to their subordinates for their acts of commission/omission that call for action against them. Explanation of the individual concerned is sought by way of issue of a show cause notice to him in regard to his responsibility or involvement in a lapse. Senior officers holding the appointment of Corps Commanders and above are authorised to give censures in the form of displeasure which may either take the form of a recordable or non-recordable censure. The former stays in the dossier of an officer for a specified period of three years. Such a course can be adopted for non-grave breaches or those lapses that are in the nature of a supervisory fault on the part of an officer. It could also be made use of when the lapse comes to light later and has become time barred under period of limitation.

The Indian Supreme Court, in the case of Union of India Vs Brigadier J S Sivia (Supreme Court Civil Appeal No. 1321 of 1991, order dated 25 April 1995), had examined the legality of the award of censure. The Court held, "It is obvious from various documents that the award of censure is being regulated by customs of service. There is resonable basis to assume that the award of censure is being governed by the 'custom of service. . . . keeping in view the status, responsibility and functions of the Chief of the Army Staff, it would be permissible for him under law to issue Army Orders from time to time for the maintenance of discipline and keeping control of the Army which is under his command."

Compensation

The modes enumerated so far related to sanctions that can be inflicted on individuals. But how do we proceed against a State? Is there any mode by which sanctions can be inflicted in a meaningful way on a State? According to Protocol I, Article 91, "A Party to the conflict which violates the provisions of the Conventions, or of this Protocol shall, if the case demands, be liable to pay compensation. It shall be responsible for all acts committed by persons forming part of its armed forces." Thus, quasi-civil sanctions may be imposed on a State to pay compensation for the damage it has caused. A recourse to order payment of compensation is meant to complement the mechanism of penal prosecution. Obligation devolves upon a State to pay the amount ordered as compensation. In turn it would induce its concerned instrumentality (the armed forces) to adhere to the accepted norms of human rights and humanitarian laws to avoid such contingencies. In this manner, the mode of compensation would generate indirect pressure on the troops to abide by laid down provisions of laws of war.

According to the prevalent practice when killing of a person is not legally justifiable, compensation may be paid to the dependents of the persons killed. Usually the Government announces payment of compensation on *ad hoc* basis. The National Human Rights Commission has started a practice of awarding compensation in cases brought to its notice. The higher judiciary has also, in a number of such situations, awarded compensation to those who suffer on account of violation of their Fundamental Rights. This provision has been found to be quite effective in providing monetary relief to the dependents of victims who have suffered at the hands of soldiers.

In the Naga People's Movement of Human Rights Vs Union of India, Writ Petition (Criminal) No. 550 of 1982 (decided on 27 November 1997), the Indian Supreme Court proceeded to firmly entrench the concept of compensation. The Court paved the way for institution of criminal action against the offenders while simultaneously giving monetary relief to the victims. The five Judges Bench held that, "in order that the people may feel assured that there is an effective check against misuse or abuse of powers by the members of the armed forces it is necessary that a complaint containing an allegation about misuse or abuse of the powers (conferred under the Armed Forces (Special Powers) Act, 1958) should be thoroughly inquired into and, if it is found that there is substance in the allegation, the victim should be suitably compensated by the State and the requisite sanction (under Section 6 of the said Act) should be granted for the institution of the prosecution and/or a civil suit or other proceeding against the person/persons responsible for such violation." It deserves to be noted that the award of compensation was not in lieu of prosecution and it did not, in any way, grant immunity to the offenders from criminal prosecution for their alleged lapses.

Adequate case law is now available on the matter of grant of compensation to the victims who have suffered at the hands of to armed forces. In the case of Charanjit Kaur Vs Union of India, AIR 1994 SC 1491, the responsibility for the death of an Army officer was prima facie traceable to an act of criminal ommission and commission on the part of the concerned authorities. His widow, the petitioner, was held to be entitled to suitable compensation of rupees six lakh as well as to the special family pension and the children allowance. The case of Sepoy Bhuwaneshwar Singh Vs Union of India, 1993 Criminal Law Journal Page 3454 (Supreme Court) is relevant. A High Court had decided to award a sum of rupees 1,000 for illegal detention in military custody. The Supreme Court enhanced the sum to rupees 30,000. It opined that, "The payment of compensation in such cases is not to be understood, as it is generally understood in a civil action, for damages under the private law, but in the broader sense of providing relief by an order of making monetary amends under the public law for the wrong done due to breach of public duty, in not protecting the Fundamental Rights of the citizen. The compensation is in the nature of exemplary damages awarded against the wrongdoer for the breach of its public law duty."

Another interesting case related to a matter where Calcutta High Court took notice of accidental death of a civilian in course of fire works display by the army personnel at a rowing club function. A criminal case was registered against the army authorities. The police was asked to submit an enquiry report. Subsequently, the High Court chose to ensure that the wife of the victim was offered suitable employment, other concessions and facilities besides a one time monetary help of rupees 12 lakh. The court ordered that no prosecution or criminal case would continue with regard to the above death. It recalled the need to uphold social and economic justice, a basic structure of the Constitution and termed its own judgement as a case of "rehabilitory justice." (Order dated 13 July 1998 in Calcutta High Court WP No. 12902 (W) of 1997). Such a judgement could provide a basis for securing beneficial relief when cited as a precedent by the victims who have suffered consequent to the operations undertaken by the armed forces.

Safeguards and Judicial Gurantees

It has been provided under the Conventions that persons accused of grave breaches shall benefit by safeguards of proper trial and defence, which shall not be less favourable than those provided in Article 105 and those following of the Geneva Convention relative to treatment of prisoners of war. (I, 49; II, 50; III, 129 and IV, 146).

The accused is always human. The accused persons must, despite the reprobation felt for violations of laws of war, have the full benefit of jurisdictional and procedural guarantees. Army Act is a self contained code. Adequate procedural safeguards have been provided under the Army Act, Rules framed thereunder and the Regulations to an accused with a view to enable him to defend himself effectively during the disciplinary process. There are certain golden rules that are invariably followed. Firstly, an accused is presumed to be innocent till proved otherwise. Secondly, the onus of proving the charge against him beyond all reasonable doubt rests upon the prosecution. Thirdly, the trial cannot proceed in the absence of the accused. No one can be compelled to be a witness against himself. Lastly, the benefit of doubt shall always be given to him. Indian Constitution prohibits retrospective application of criminal laws and double jeopardy. Army Act provides immunity from double punishment.

The Rules stipulate that an accused is entitled at all times to consult the Judge Advocate during the passage of trial on any points concerning the law relating to the charge or the procedure. An accused is provided due opportunity to defend himself. He is entitled to engage a counsel to represent him. He also gets the benefit of a friend of the accused or a defending officer to assist him in his defence. He is entitled to uncensored correspondence and access to his lawyers. When charged with an offence punishable with death, persons below officer ranks may seek help of a civil counsel at the Government expense to appear for them at the court martial. Court Martial proceedings usually take place in open court. The provisions of the Indian Evidence Act are fully applicable. Though there is no provision to enlarge an accused on bail, the mode of arrest can be changed from close arrest to open arrest when he can get greater freedom of movement. On compassionate grounds grant of leave of absence may also be considered for an accussed. By and large, the Army Rules afford equal opportunities for putting up his defence to an accused when compared to the Criminal Procedure Code which is applicable to his civilian counterparts. To achieve fair play and impartiality in administration of justice, effective steps have been taken to minimise the element of command influence in rendering advice for disposal of disciplinary cases. Different legal advisers are entrusted with the handling of a disciplinary case at the pre-trial, trial and post-trial stages.

Relevant Case Law

So far the legal practitioners do not have the benefit of judicial pronouncements with respect to various provisions of IHL. The judicial philosophy is, however, laid bare from a number of judgements where the Courts have dealt with the matters relating to injuries or damage caused during employment of troops. The Supreme Court of India has, in a landmark judgement, extensively dwelt on the role and scope of the authority available to the army personnel while operating under the Armed Forces (Special Powers) Act, 1958 (herein after called the Central Act). This Act is somewhat on the same lines as the Reserve Forces Act, 1980 of UK. In the Naga People's case supra the petitioners had alleged wide spread abuse of powers by the armed forces personnel while the forces were deployed in the areas declared as 'disturbed areas' under the Central Act. Refuting the allegations, the respondents had placed before the Supreme Court instructions in the form of a list of "Do's and Don'ts" that were issued by the Army Headquarters from time to time. All soldiers deployed in the 'disturbed areas' were expected to carry the one page manual in their pocket. They had been asked to abide by its contents in letter and spirit. It was argued that these instructions provided an effective check against any misuse or abuse of the powers conferred under the Central Act on a military officer. Contravention of these instructions was claimed to be punishable under Senctions 41, 42(e), 63 and 64(7) of the Army Act.

The Apex Court went on to examine the legality of such executive instructions in the form of "Do's and Don'ts". It also had a close look at their contents. Having regard to the former, the Supreme Court held that, "when rules itself do not contain any guidelines, directions or criteria, the instructions issued by the Government furnish an essential and statutory procedure for the purpose of securing uniformity in application of the rules. These instructions really fill up the yawning gaps in the provisions and are embeded in the conditions of service. These are binding on the Government and cannot be violated to the prejudice of the Government servant." The Court opined that, "The actual practice, being in conformity with the constitutional scheme, should also be awarded legal sanction by permissible constitutional interpretation."

Adverting to the legality of the "Do's and Don'ts" *per-se* the Supreme Court held that "these are binding instructions which are required to be followed by the members of the armed forces exercising powers under the Central Act and a serious note should be taken of violation of the instructions and the persons found responsible for such violations should be suitably punished under the Army Act, 1950." The Supreme Court, further in the same judgement, directed incorporation of a few safeguards against an arbitrary exercise of powers to bring them (Do's and Dont's) in line with the guidelines contained in its decision in that regard.

Protectionism

Apprehension is sometimes expressed about the practicability of prosecutions of the armed forces personnel for IHL violations. Such fear is said to be based on the grounds of protectionism. In support of such an hypothesis it is stated that Section 6 of the Armed Forces (Special Powers) Act, 1958 provides protection to such men in uniform. The section goes to prescribe, "No prosecution, suit or other legal proceedings shall be instituted against any person in respect of anything done or purported to be done in exercise of the powers conferred by the said Act except with the previous sanction of the Central Government." The conferment of such a protection has been assailed on the gound that it virtually provides immunity to persons exercising special powers of firing or using force, destroying dumps, arrest and search without warrant etc; in as much as it extends the protection also to "anything purported to be done in exercise of the powers conferred by this Act."

In one of the cases mentioned above it was argued that adequate protection for members of armed forces from arrest and prosecution is available in Sections 45 and 197 of the Criminal Procedure Code. Hence, a separate provision like the one contained in Section 6 *ibid* giving further protection is not called for. It was also pointed out that even if sanction for prosecution is granted, the person in question would be able to plead a statutory defence in criminal proceedings under the pleas of good faith and mistake of fact/law.

The above arguments were duly considered by the Supreme Court of India in the Naga People's case supra. The Court held, "the protection given under Section 6 (of the Central Act) cannot be regarded as conferment of an immunity on the persons exercising the powers under the said Act. It only gives protection in the form of previous sanction of the Central Gevernment before a criminal prosecution or a suit or other civil proceeding is instituted against such a person. It has to be borne in mind that a discretionary power is not necessarily a discriminatory power and that abuse of power is not to be easily assumed where discretion is vested in the Government and not in a minior official. . . ." At the same time to guard against any possibility of abuse of authority by the Government from such interpretation, the Court preceeded to institute a balance. It said, "since the order of the Central Government refusing or granting the sanction under Section 6 is subject to judicial review, the Central Government shall pass an order giving reasons."

Apprehension may also be expressed about likelihood of a commission of crime being defended on the ground of military necessity. Such a fear does not appear to be well founded. The Defence Services Regulations highlight two important principles viz use of minimum force and need to act in good faith which are to be scrupulously followed by the troops while deployed in aid to civil authorities. Observance of these two principles would ensure that unnecessary and avoidable injuries or damage are not caused. In so far as war like situations go, one of the principles of war viz economy of efforts similarly comes into play. It calls for use of only the required amount of force to achieve the military objective assigned to the troops. These principles would negate and counter any likelihood to take shelter behind the plea of military necessity to justify use of excessive force.

Military Manuals

Military manuals indicate the national interpretation of various problems related to IHL. A simple soldier may not be able to grasp the implications of texts contained in documents of ratification. Hence, the utility of manuals serve as a basic tool of reference for the military lawyers whose task is to advise commanders about the laws of armed conflict. Manuals are apt to develop national understanding which is of practical relevance. Such manuals also indicate the status of implementation in various countries.

In India a comprehensive and informative manual of IHL provisions is yet to be produced. The Manual of Military Law in its three volumes and the Regulations for the Army (in two volumes) contains a compendium of statutes, rules and ordinances of reference utility to the armed forces personnel. Yet these five volumes have not dealt with IHL provisions at all.

The training of military personnel in certain schools of instructions involves lessons on Geneva Conventions and Protocols. ICRC publications are made use of by the military law instructors. There is a definite need for proper manuals, pamphlets and precis to be produced besides a comprehensive commentary that could also present the available case law concerning national practices of other States.

A handy pictorical booklet on "Rules for Behaviour in Combat" was brought out jointly by the Judge Advocate General's Department and the Indian Red Cross Society in 1986. It depicted very lucidly some basic rules of conduct to be observed by soldiers during armed conflicts. It was a bilingual publication being in English and Hindi. In its foreword, the Chief of the Army Staff had written that he expected every soldier to be conversant with these Rules so that he not only follows them implicily but is also vigilant against their violation by others. The contents of the above booklet are shown in Table 5.

Thereafter during 1994 in the wake of increased deployment of Indian Army in low intensity conflict situations, the Army Headquarters had caused to be published a one page manual titled *"COAS Commandments"*. Its text is contained in Table 6.

Subsequently during the Vigyan Bhawan Seminar held in New Delhi during August 1996 a small booklet titled *Rules of Behaviour in Combat* was released. Its publication was a joint exercise by the offices of Judge Advocate General (Army) and the Regional Delegate of the ICRC, New Delhi. This carried a one page directive bearing signatures of the then Chief of Army Staff. This was titled "Mandate of the COAS about personal behaviour and conduct in operations." Its contents are shown in Table 7.

The Supreme Court had the occasion to critically examine the contents of the above mandate during Naga People's case supra. The Court suggested a few amendments to be inserted so as to provide further safeguards as discussed above.

Besides the one page manual indicated above the Army Training Notes are issued by the Directorate General of Military Training at the Army Headquarters. These Notes elaborately deal with the question of proportionality in the use of force when the troops are requisitioned by the civil authorities to maintain public order. One of the principles and rules given a clear warning that in case the force used was disproportionate or excessive, the person ordering use of such force may face legal action if it is established that there was lack of due care and attention.

India's Concern

India has an international border extending about 16,000 kilometers. It has a coast line of 7,600 kilometers and an exclusive economic zone of 2.2 million square kilometers. It has maritime boundaries with Indonesia, Malaysia, Thailand, Myanmar, Sri Lanka, Maldives, Pakistan and Bangladesh.

There have been a number of wars fought on the Indian sub continent in the last fifty years. Casualty figures on the Indian side and also of the opposing forces during these armed conflicts and the proxy war are shown in the Tables 8 to 14. Therefore, Indian armed forces have a visible and real concern for understanding and adherence to the Conventions and Protocols. India's commitment to the observance of laws of war is genuine and inescapable. Such a requirement becomes further manifest considering the frequent employment of Indian contingents in UN Peace Keeping Missions during armed conflicts in different regions of the world. A list of operations where Indian troops have been employed for Peace keeping activities are shown in Table 15. Soldiers who are properly aware of the mandate of IHL would alone be able to efficiently discharge tha task assigned to them of restoring peace.

Recommendations

26th International Conference of the Red Cross and Red Crescent held at Geneva in 1995 in its report titled *International Humanitarian Law: From Law to Action* had presented a few concrete, effective and thoughtful recommendations. In tune with the same, the suggestions made in this presentation are listed below. It is clarified that the recommendations made are general in nature and based on a global perspective. Considering its own domestic policies and international legal obligations a State may wish to decide whether or not it would like to ratify a particular instrument of humanitarian law. Fully conscious of such a vital contemporary reality, the suggested recommendations aim to be highly advantageous for over all refinement of military law approach for the prosecution of IHL violations.

(a) Laws governing the Army, Navy and the Air Force could be suitably amended so that effective penalties are prescribed by the way of penal sanctions for breaches of the Conventions by bringing them within the list of military offences. (I, 49; II, 50; III, 129; IV, 146). Appropriate provisions should be inserted in the model law to be drafted so that such breaches could relate to the offences with ragard to refugees, hostages and civilians etc. An omnibus section could be inserted which may relate to breaches of Geneva Conventions and the Protocols. The heading of such a section may read as 'Violations of IHL Provisions'.

(b) Specific penalty should be allotted for each of the grave and other breaches. The punishments laid down for various breaches should have a similarity as regards those suggested by the Conventions and also in the national legislations enacted by various States for uniform implementation of humanitarian laws.

(c) More precise and common rules relating to attempt, abetment and conspiracy need to be adopted.

(d) The term 'combatant' needs to be defined in the statutory laws and regulations.

(e) Necessary legislation to ensure mutual legal assistance and co-operation in extradition should be adopted in peace time.

(f) Dissemination activities should be developed at various levels of rank structure of the military forces. This is a permanent obligation. (I, 47; II, 48; III, 127; IV, 144). It would cater for urgent and ongoing need to convince present and potential perpetrators of violence that they should respect humanitarian principles.

(g) Legal advisors for military leaders should be employed and duly trained. Qualified personnel who are properly trained would facilitate the implementation of the Conventions. This should be arranged on a permanent basis.

(h) The training of the armed forces in international humanitarian law should be given added emphasis. IHL is applied by soldiers from the highest rank of Field Marshal down to the lowest Sepoy. Dissemination should be carried out in national languages and the texts translated in Hindi so that they can be applied by the population and be easily understood.

(i) Text editions of all relevant Conventions should be prepared and military manuals published so that these can be read and understood by the armed forces personnel. Military manuals may be drafted to conform to the generally accepted approach of humanitarian norms expected in combat. The manuals should be brought out separately for use by the officers, medical personnel, legal advisors and soldiers. A modern standard treatise of the Conventions and Protocols should also be developed with extensive foot notes, commentary and case law. The Advisory Service of the ICRC could play a co-ordinating role in this regard. Particular care needs to be taken with regard to the drafting of the text. These manuals would present an opportunity to include national interpretations of various issues. Military lawyers would then be able to suitably advise commanders at the appropriate level on the application of Conventions and about the laws of armed conflict.

(j) Compilation of national case law should be undertaken and detailed analysis carried out by military law experts in consultation with the Advisory Service of the ICRC to identify areas warranting drafting, adoption and amendment to the legislation in the sphere of definition of offences and procedural law.

Prosecution and punishments of individuals acting in their private capacity would normally remain a matter for the domestic courts possessing jurisdiction and custody. Suitable amendments to the military laws would make it more effective and potent to deal with violations of war crimes. Publication of an uptodate manual for the armed forces and a commentary of the Conventions and Protocols would facilitate dissemination and easy assimilation of the provisions by the men in uniform. In cases where domestic approach is not feasible the proposed International Criminal Court would hopefully come forward to implement the concept of universal application of international criminal law to all offenders regardless of affiliation, status or nationality.

TABLE NO. 1

Relevant Provisions of Indian Constitution

Article	Subject Matter
32.	Remedies for Enforcement of Fundamental Rights
34.	Restriction of Fundamental Rights While Martial Law is in Force
39.	Equal Justice and Free Legal Aid
51.	Promotion of Internal Peace and Security

TABLE NO. 2
Offences Under the Act

Statement of Offence under the Army Act	Breaches of Law of Wars (Example)	Army Act Section	Maximum Punishment (Years of Imprison-ment)
1. Breaking into any house or other place in search of plunder	Appropriation of property	36 (b)	14 on active service, otherwise 7 years
2. Disobedience of a lawful command		41	14
3. Unbecoming conduct	Making perfidious use of the protective emblem	45	Cashiering
4. Disgraceful conduct of a cruel kind	(a) Inhuman treatment (b) Willfully causing great suffeing	46	7
5. Extortion	Taking of hostage	53	10
6. An Act/Omission prejudicial to good order and military discipline	(a) Torture (b) Inhuman treatment (c) Biological experiments	63	7
7. Defiling of place of worship or intentionally wounding religious feeling of any person	Attacking and causing destruction of places of worship	64 (b)	7
8. Committing an offence against the property or person of any inhabitant or resident of the country in which serving	(a) Attacking and causing destruction of historic monuments, works of art etc. (b) Destruction of property	64 (f)	7

TABLE NO. 3

Different Modes of Investigation at Pre Trial Stage

1. Court of Inquiry under the Army Rules
2. Report sought by the National Human Rights Commission
3. Inquiry conducted by a Commission of Inquiry

TABLE NO. 4

Various Modes of Disciplinary Action Under the Military Law for Violations of IHL

1. Courts Martial
2. Summary Trial
3. Summary Disposal
4. Penal Deductions
5. Administrative Action
   (a) Termination of Service
   (b) Termination of Service without issue of a Show Cause Notice
   (c) Award of Censure
      (i) Recordable
      (ii) Non-Recordable
6. Compensation by way of a Public Claim

TABLE NO. 5

Contents of Rules for Behaviour in Combat

Combatants

1. Fight only combatants
2. Attack only military targets
3. Spare civilian persons and objects
4. Restrict destruction to what your mission requires

Enemy Combatants and Surrender

1. Spare them
2. Disarm them
3. Treat them humanely
4. Hand them over to your superior

Wounded Enemy Combatants

1. Collect them
2. Care for them
3. Hand them over to your superior
4. Or to the nearest medical personnel

Civilian Persons

1. Respect them
2. Treat those in your power humanely
3. Protect them against ill-treatment. Vengeance and taking of hostages and prohibited
4. Respect their property; do not damage it or steal it

(Contd. . .)

Distinctive Signs

1. Respect persons bearing and objects marked with such signs
2. Let these persons perform their tasks, if not ordered otherwise
3. Leave these buildings, establishment monuments untouched and do not enter them, if not ordered otherwise.
4. Let these vehicles, ships and aircrafts move and do not enter them, if not ordered otherwise

TABLE NO. 6

Coas Commandments

1. No Rape
2. No Molestation
3. No Torture
4. No Military Disgrace i.e. loss of arms/mil post or surrender or imbibing of un-army like culture
5. No Medling in Civ Adm i.e. land disputes or quarrels
6. Competence in PL/Coy Tactics with Innovations
7. Willingly Carry out Civic Action with Innocations
8. Develop Media Interaction Modus - Use it as a 'force multiplier' and not as a 'force degrader'
9. Respect Human Rights
10. Only fear God, uphold Dharma (Ethical mode of life - the path of righteousness) and enjoy serving the country

TABLE NO. 7

Mandate of the COAS About Personal Behaviour & Conduct in Operations

1. Do your duty fearlessly - the Army is with you
2. Conduct all operations with minimum but adquate force, in accordance with the laid down battle drills and procedures
3. Rape and molestation are the most heinous of crimes. God will not forgive you, and the Army will punish your very severely
4. Compassion towards the population in the area of operation - do what you can to lessen the trauma of civil population
5. Be polite to civil population during cordons and searches
6. Their property must be protected, looting and destroying it are criminal acts
7. Rape, molestation, murder, taking of hostage and arbitrary executions are violations of humanitarian law
8. You will be punished severely for violations of above directions
9. Follow established code of conduct and behaviour amongst member nations of the world in any armed conflict
10. Remember - *"Dharam, Iman and Sharafat"*. (The path of righteousness, conscience and decency)

TABLE NO. 8

Operations in Jammu & Kashmir (1947-48) Casualty Figures

	Indian Army Killed	Wounded	**J & K State** Forces	**RIAF**
Officers	76	81		
JCOs	31	107		
Other Ranks	996	2964		
Total	1103	3152		
			1990 Killed, Wounded and Missing Presumed to Be Dead	32 Officers and Men

Pakistan

Total 20,000 Including 6000 Killed

Source: "Red Coats to Olive Green, History of Indian Army (1600-1974)", by Longer V; New Delhi, 1974, Page 317.

TABLE NO. 9

Operation Polo In Hyderabad, 1948 Casualty Figures

Indian Army	
Killed	10
Razakars	
Killed and Wounded	1200
Captured	450

Source: "Red Coats to Olive Green, A History of Indian Army (1600-1974)" by Longer V; New Delhi, 1974, Page 322.

TABLE NO. 10

Liberation of Goa, December 1961 Casualty Figures

	Indians		Portugese
	JCOs	Or	
Killed	1	3	10
Wounded	1	13	2
Prisioners			
Officers			24
Soldiers			544
Police			9
Local Police			268
Civilians			8
Total			853

Source: Operation Vijay by P N Khera, A Publication of Historical Section, Ministry of Defence, Government of India, Page 103.

TABLE 11
Sino Indian War, 1962: Casualties

	Killed	Wounded
Indian	1400	1700
Chinese	---------- Total 8000 ---------	

Source: Brassey's Battles by John Laffin, 1986.

TABLE NO. 12

Indo-Pak War, 1965: Casualty Figures

	Killed	Wounded	Missing
INDIA			
Officers		436	
JCOs		347	
Other Ranks		7768	
Total	2862	8617	1507
PAKISTAN			
Killed	1033		

Source: Report on the Health of the Armed Forces Page 37-39; As quoted in History of Indo-Pak War, 1965; a publication of Historical Section, Ministry of Defence, Government of India, Page 320.

TABLE NO. 13

Indo-Pak War 1971 Casualty Figures

	Eastern Command	Western Command	Southern Command
INDIA			
Killed			
Officers	68	84	7
JCOs	62	61	7
Other Ranks	1348	1285	76
Total	1478	1430	90
Missing			
Officers	-	19	2
JCOs	4	22	-
Other Ranks	43	791	15
Total	47	832	17

(Contd. . .)

(Contd. . .)

	Eastern Command	Western Command	Southern Command
Wounded			
Officers	207	162	23
JCOs	169	111	7
Other Ranks	3828	3257	222
Total	4204	3530	252
Grand Total	5729	5792	359
Total Army Casualties = 11,880			
NAVY			
Officers	20		
Sailors	180		
Total	200		
AIR FORCE			
Total	109		

PAKISTAN

Killed			
Regulars	6761		
Para Military Fofces	1628		
Total	8389	3730	336
NAVY			
Total	485		
AIR FORCE			
Total	Not Known		
Wounded			
Regular	8000		
Para Military Forces	988		
Total	8988	11302	97

- 74,000 Military and Para Military Personnel Surrendered in Eastern Command
- 554 Soldiers Captured by Indian Troops

Source: "History of Indo Pak War, 19[illegible] art II, Page 687-88, published by Historical Section, Ministry of Defence, Government of India."

TABLE NO. 14

Result of the Army Operations - J&K 1990-1998

Year	Militants Killed	Militants Apprehended	Militants Surrendered	Weapons Recovered
1990	446	3267	37	1691
1991	632	2973	138	2196
1992	637	4089	226	3153
1993	1042	3405	73	2516
1994	1228	3197	128	2733
1995	1102	3541	657	3313
1996	902	1826	224	2274
1997	888	1257	235	1997
Total	**6897**	**23555**	**1718**	**19873**
1998				
January	36	56	4	101
February	41	45	14	106
March	43	74	10	99
April	54	26	5	175
May	32	36	8	110
June	60	20	7	99
July	117	25	8	166
August*	30	5	-	33
Total	**413**	**287**	**56**	**894**
Grand Total	**7310**	**23842**	**1774**	**20767**

* Till 10 August, 1998

Source: *Sainik Samachar*, 1-15 September, 1998, page 13.

TABLE NO. 15

Employment of Indian Armed Forces in UN Peace Keeping Missions

S. No.	Name/Location of Mission	Period	Strength
1.	Korea	1953-54	6000 infantry
2.	Cambodia	1954-58	Member, Supervisory Commission
3.	Laos	1964-68	Medical detachment
4.	Vietnam	1954-70	7000 troops to Supervisory Commission
5.	UNEF (Sinai)	1956-67	Two Force Commanders and 11 battalions of infantry
6.	UNOGIL (Lebanon)	1958	Observers
7.	ONUC (Congo)	1960-64	The first multi-role PKO; 12000 troops
8.	UNYOM (Yemen)	1963	A Force Commander and Observers
9.	UNFICYP (Cyprus)	1964 onwards	Three Force Commanders
10.	DOMREP (Dominican Republic)	1965	SG's Military Adviser
11.	UNIIMOG (Iran-Iraq)	1987	Observers
12.	UNAVEM (Angola)	1988	Observers

(Contd. . .)

(Contd. . .)

S. No.	Name/Location of Mission	Period	Strength
13.	UNTAG (Namibia)	1978-89	A Force Commander, Observers, Police Monitors, Electoral Supervisors
14.	ONUCA (Central America)	1989	Observers
15.	ONUSAL (El Salvador)	1991	Observers
16.	UNIKOM (Iraq-Kuwait)	1991	Observers
17.	UNOMIL (Liberia)	1991	Observers
18.	UNPROFOR (Former Yugoslavia)	1992	First Force Commander
19.	UNTAC (Cambodia)	1992	Infantry, Observers, Electoral Supervisors
20.	ONUMOZ (Mozambique)	1992	Infantry
21.	UNOSOM (Somalia)	1993-95	Infantry
22.	UNAMIR (Rwanda)	1994	Infantry
23.	UNAVEM (Angola)	1995	Infantry

Bibliography

A Brief Outline of International Humanitarian Law, by Stanislaw E Nahalik.

Administrative Law by Prof SP Sathe, 5th Edition.

Asia Pacific Defence Forum, Fall 1995.

Beating the Backlog : Speeding up Wheels of Justice by Dr Abhishek Singhvi.

Commentary on Convention IV, Part IV, Execution of the Convention — Section 1, General Provisions — Penal Sanctions.

Commentary on Penal Sanctions that should be Implemented for Breaches and Violations of International Law of Armed Conflicts, by Claudio Santorum.

Constitution and Practice of Court Martial by Thomas Fredrick Simmons, Esq, 1873 Edition.

Dissemination of IHL Provisions to Armed Forces, by Brig Nilendra Kumar.

Education and Youth in a Democratic Society by N A Palkhivala.

Freedom of Information by Justice V R Krishna Iyer (Retd).

Hand Book of Military Law by Capt R J Wilkins and WS Chaney.

Human Rights and Human Diversity by A J M Milne.

Human Rights and the Law by Paras Diwan & Peeyushi Diwan.

Human Rights in Changing World by Antonica Cassese.

Human Rights : Perspective and Challenges in 1990 and Beyond.

Human Rights from Rhetoric to Reality by Tom Campbell.

ICRC - Annual Report, 1997.

Implementing International Humanitarian Law, by Yves Sandoz.

Implementing International Humanitarian Law: Problems and Priorities, by Dieter Fleck.

Judgements and How to Write Them by Justice S D Singh.

Justice for the Common Man by A K Sen, M C Setalvad and G S Pathak.

Law, Judges and Justice by S M N Raina.

Manual of Military Law, Part I, 1972, published by Ministry of Defence, London.

Military Mobile Education by Cmdr Juno Jamison.

National Measures to Implement International Humanitarian Law, ICRC, Geneva, October 1991.

National Measures for the Implementation of IHL - The Geneva Conventions Act, 1960, A Study, by M K Balachandran.

Resurrection, A Human Right in India by R C Jha.

Report Containing Practices of India Concerning Himanitarian Law Applicable in Times of Armed Conflict, by Dr N L Mitra and Dr U V Kadam.

Report titled International Humanitarian Law, From Law to Action of the 26th International Concerence of the Red Cross and Red Crescent, held at Geneva during December 1995.

Role of the Armed Forces in Promotion of Human Rights by General Barry R Mc Caffrey.

The Law of War Crimes — National and International Approaches, by Timothy L H McCormack and Gerry J Simpson.

The Penal Repression of Violations of International Humanitarian Law Applicable to Non-International Armed Conflicts, by Denise Plattner.

Shorter Constitution of India by Dr D D Basu, 12th Edition.

Wars of National Liberation and War Criminality.

World Human Rights Guide by Carles Humana.